Design for Modern Living

Design for Modern Living

Gerd and Ursula Hatje

With 105 plates in full colour, 395 black-and-white plates and 50 plans

Thames and Hudson London

Translated by Irene and Harold Meek

© 1961 Droemersche Verlagsanstalt Munich/Zurich
This edition © 1962 Thames & Hudson Ltd London
Illustrations printed in Germany by
Graphische Kunstanstalt Osiris Munich
Text printed in Holland by Bosch - Utrecht

Contents

Introduction

Introduction

The furnishing trade presents a bewildering picture. Wholesalers and retailers offer us an enticing array of wares. No year passes in which dozens of new designs are not created and put into production; in which new fashions are not brought on to the market with a flourish. One season the fashionable wood will be elm, only to be ousted by teak a season later. The proud possessor of lamps made from Danish glass will find himself gazing enviously at Japanese paper lamp-shades displayed in the store windows and looking every bit as desirable. In one and the same breath architects tell us that we should have an open hearth in the living room and separate living and dining areas. No sooner have we become attuned to the all-white enamel kitchen than the trend changes to pastel shades, then back to wood veneers.

There is no lack of examples, ranging from government offices and country halls, banks, company board-rooms, and hotel foyers to the newly furnished living room of our next-door neighbors. What temptations – both good and bad! Besides, every one of us has his individual demands and needs, which make it difficult if not impossible to take over lock, stock, and barrel any particular solution that we may happen to like. This family has many children, that one wants peace and quiet. One family enjoys chamber music, another wants to do a lot of entertaining, a third needs storage space for a big library; in the case of the fourth the lady adores flowers and does not want to do without them even in her upper-story apartment. Here a setting has to be contrived for antique furniture, there works of art must be displayed to their best advantage. There are so many demands to be satisfied and so many possibilities from which to choose. What is important? What is lasting?

The close observer of the contemporary scene soon discovers that despite the manifold possibilities a number of clear-cut national stylistic trends in modern living can be discerned. He will realize that these trends not only determine the shape of the individual pieces of furniture but, beyond that, the over-all character of the room. Our book illustrates many examples of this. All the pieces shown are widely available nowadays, thanks to the rami-

1

1   Hans J. Wegner. Armchair, 1949. This Danish design is an outstanding example of the Scandinavian style of furniture with its organic, sculpturesque shape. Note the swelling and tapering of the wooden parts and the contrast in texture between the smooth teak and the cane weave.

2

2   Edvard Kindt-Larsen. Easy chair, 1954. The Scandinavian mastery in handling wood-work is also apparent in their commercial mass-production methods. In this instance a special problem, that of a collapsable frame, has been solved impeccably.

3 Gio Ponti. Chair. Even in this apparently simple example of a chair the matter-of-course elegance of Italian design can be perceived at once. The ideal of visual lightness has been carried to its structural limits.

3

fications of international trade; either the original designs are imported and manufactured under license or else they are copied, not always successfully, by local producers.

For some years now, Scandinavian ideas have swept Europe and America and have earned the Danes the reputation of being leaders in the field of furniture design. Founded upon local folk art and a centuries-old craft tradition, a characteristic style of furniture was developed in Scandinavia; its forms are organic and its lines gently curved, with finely modeled wooden parts and a generally compact shape. Combined with this is a mastery in the handling of wood and an instinctive feeling for its inherently attractive character, which is allowed full play even when the articles are mass-produced. This feeling for texture manifests itself in combinations of wood, leather, canework, metal, textiles, and furs. Such furniture has been designed with small rooms in mind. It is anti-impressive; it creates a cozy atmosphere, and because of its organic shape and lightness it is often contrasted, possibly as a dining unit, with furniture of more massive proportions that requires a good deal of space. Perhaps this aptitude for combining different idioms within the general concept of furniture is one of the main attractions of the Scandinavian style, which by itself often possesses a craft-like quality. This does not, however, apply to that part of the Danish furniture industry which rejects the excessively organic types of design and prefers the international trend towards angular geometric shapes.

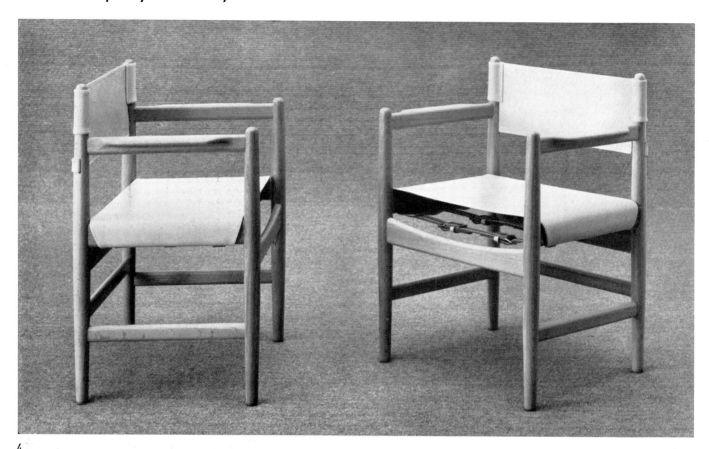

4

5

page 12:

4   Børge Mogensen. Armchair, 1955. A variation of the colonial chair frequently used in Scandinavia, whose popularity may stem not only from country style and folk influences, but also from that structural honesty which expresses the functional connections between frame and cover.

5   Poul Kjaerholm. Easy chair, 1958. In its block-like, squared-off shape, this design typifies the trend in Scandinavian style that veers towards the angular, geometric line of the international style without dispensing completely with a specifically Scandinavian character, as shown in the curved shape of the subframe.

page 13:

6   Franco Albini. Cane chair. The chalice shape of this Italian design springs from a concept of plasticity in which the flexible nature of manila cane has been fully exploited.

7   Osvaldo Borsani. Adjustable chaise-longue, 1957. The perfect mechanism of this chaise-longue, adjustable in height and inclination, is an example of the love of experiment and the imaginative technical virtuosity of many Italian furniture designers. It has unquestionably succeeded here in imbuing technical achievements with a refined elegance of form.

6

7

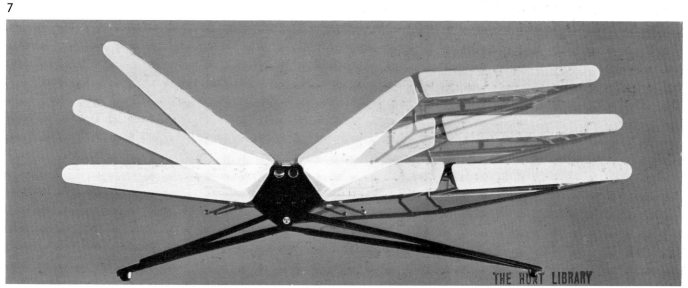

8

9

10

The Italian style of furnishing is characterized by a flair for exquisite settings, effective presentation, and genuine impressiveness. Furniture of different periods and styles, modern and antique works of art, together with various original products of native craftsmen (which are occasionally thought of as in bad taste north of the Alps) make up an ensemble in which fancy and functionalism harmoniously unite. Behind it all is a certain open-mindedness toward everything new and a readiness to assimilate and apply it usefully for one's own purposes. Individual furniture design is distinguished by elegance and a delight in experimenting with problems of form, technique, and the handling of materials. The rather sparse furnishing permits each piece to show to best advantage, allowing as it does for the scale of lofty rooms, the cool background of whitewashed walls, and the distinction of marble floors in southern houses.

The American style of living – or more precisely, what has been proclaimed as the American style of living by a dozen avant-garde (and hence devoutly modern) American furniture manufacturers and a small group of equally modern architects today-exerts an influence on the whole of Western Europe. Hence we are justified in speaking of an international style as applied to furniture of generous proportions with simple functional lines, cool elegance of shape and material (selected veneers, mat enamel and plastic surfaces, chromium-plated metal, glass, polished marble) and great precision of workmanship. Whereas until quite recently the American-international style for the most part used geometric shapes based on cubes, rectangles, and circles, resulting in an angular block-like appearance, important new designs have in the last few years been inspired by organic forms. This is particularly the case where plastics have been used. An equally important factor is undoubtedly the American stress on the practical demands of modern living. In the matter of achieving perfection of kitchen and household, in the adaptation of plan and furnishings to a changed mode of living, and in the ability to combine economic and aesthetic needs harmoniously, American examples have been copied the world over.

8 Eero Saarinen. Easy chair, 1947. Organic shapes are readily achieved in designs based on the pliability of new materials. The seat of this softly contoured chair consists of a molded plastic material covered with foam rubber.

9 Charles Eames. Chair, 1952. The metal frame, which despite its apparent complication is of light appearance, carries an upholstered wire basket. Technical necessities have been exploited to aesthetic ends.

10 Florence Knoll. Easy chair, 1955. The severe angularity and precision of the steel section, typical of a certain range of American furniture, have been combined with a shaped backrest to create a comfortable sitting position.

However diverse the individual styles of our time may appear, they can be traced back to a common root. Modern furnishing styles are not the natural result of a unbroken historical development in the way that the Baroque developed from Renaissance or Rococo from Baroque; they were initiated rather by individual designs made by certain pioneers. The nineteenth century had led to a decline in standards of taste. The new social strata which resulted from increasing industrialization – the working class recruited for the most part from the rural population, and the upper middle classes with their rapidly mounting prosperity – gave rise to problems which remained unsolved. For the first time in Western history man proved unequal to the task of adapting his environment to his requirements. The stuffy and un-inhabitable houses were as chaotic and depressing as the enormous, dirty industrial suburbs. Together with this inability to evolve a new style went a growing desire for ostentation. Every middle-class home had its little-used 'drawing-room' and every apartment house, mostly decorated with a Ba-roque or Renaissance façade, had its living rooms overlooking the street, even if this meant a sunless northern prospect. Inside the rooms was period furniture – neo-Gothic, Italian Renaissance, Baroque, Rococo. The windows were hung with heavy curtains which caught the dust, while all was shrouded in picturesque shadows. Colors were confined to dingy monotones. In more demanding interiors, which were designed by artists in the so-called studio style, composition and arrangement took no account of people and their needs. But even in the 'good room' of modest houses the round table

11

11 Ludwig Mies van der Rohe. Barcelona Chair, 1929. This chair, designed by Mies van der Rohe for the German Pavilion at the World's Fair in Barcelona 1929, has an impressive elegance that remains unsurpassed in the modern furniture industry. Its extraordinary aesthetic quality depends upon the structural lines and the contrast between organic material (leather) and inorganic material (chromium-plated steel).

with its four or six high-backed chairs would almost always occupy the center of the room. These rooms did not consider their inhabitants; human beings were literally pushed aside.

Resistance to this type of development varied in intensity from country to country. In Scandinavia, which later rightly assumed the leadership in many questions of interior design, the tradition of solid peasant furniture was strong enough to inspire new ideas. In England, where huge sprawling cities had grown up in the coal-mining districts, and where the Great Exhibition of 1851 represented a highlight in the nineteenth-century carnival of styles, reformers such as Ruskin, Morris, or Voysey could fall back on the still-living tradition of the English country house. Precise craftsmanship and honest use of furnishing materials; simple, often box-like shapes; light furniture and bright colors; plans that develop from the inside outward, and where the position of the rooms determines the appearance of the façade; even such definite details as the incorporation of the staircase into the living room or stepped levels in a single story: such are the trends which England carried over from the nineteenth to the twentieth century (14). Morris' immediate successors abandoned the hostile attitude toward technology implicit in his praise of real craftsmanship. They had to do so, because their progressive designs could gain currency only through recourse to the media of the modern industrial age. Even then, it proved a long road to the industrial mass production of beautifully shaped and functional articles for daily use. Bentwood chairs shaped under steam, a process patented by the German Michael Thonet in 1856, have remained unmatched for their lightness and clean lines. They are still accepted today as a happy combination of elegance, practicality, and economy in manufacture (15).

Functionalism, as this over-all practicality came to be called, became a popular catchword and played a major role in the theories of modern form. The term has been interpreted in the most varied ways but it has invariably implied the rejection of stylistic imitation. The point of departure was not a certain historic shape such as a Chippendale chair, a Louis XV *fauteuil*, or a Baroque cabinet, but an investigation of the functions involved. How can a chair, an armchair, or a settee be best developed to conform with human posture; how can the process of manufacture be most honestly revealed; how can it most convincingly express the feeling for shape and the sensibility of both its designer and its owner? Whether the word 'function' was applied to intent, to manufacturing process, or to a psychological and social situation, the argument behind it was always a moral one. It was a matter of honesty and sincerity: no more borrowed styles that were out of keeping with the realities of modern life, no more unjustified desire to make a social impression such as the overbearing magnificence of 'antique' furniture had blatantly proclaimed, no pretence of craftsmanship when ornaments and moldings were merely mass-produced.

In Germany the Deutsche Werkbund led the way in the pioneer efforts at reform. The Werkbund aimed at good design in all industrial products from cutlery to houses. It found a precedent for this in the work of the Jugendstil movement (the German equivalent of Art Nouveau), which had aimed at designing everything from clothes to the house itself. But the Werkbund did not want art for the few: it wanted decent quality for all. The Jugendstil had made every weekday into a festive one. The Werkbund did not disavow weekdays, but it did want to promote design that was adapted to the needs and possibilities of the industrial age. Its aim, according to the program of 1910, was to 'create a rallying point for all who regarded industrial work as a part – and not the least part – of general cultural endeavor'.

The activities of the Werkbund were continued most effectively by the Bauhaus, and its influence spread. Founded in 1919 by Walter Gropius at Weimar and later moved to Dessau, the Bauhaus was a college of design for products of every kind, especially industrial, a school where architecture was understood to be the all-embracing art. The Bauhaus incorporated industrial manufacturing requirements into its aesthetic program. The

12 Louis Comfort Tiffany. Hamilton Fish residence, New York, about 1880. The nineteenth century was obsessed by the fear of empty space. Every corner of the room is cluttered up with furniture and *objets d'art;* thick ornament encumbers every surface. In these rooms, which are designed by one of the best known interior decorators of the end of the nineteenth century, things lead an existence of their own, as if the home were merely a museum to house a large number of precious-looking pieces of furniture. Modern houses are alive because of the activities of their inhabitants, to whom they allow freedom of movement.

13 In contrast to the clutter of many isolated objects amounting to a labyrinth in their total effect, every item in this contemporary living room is related to the others without losing its own individuality. The outline and structure of each piece remain clearly visible. If works of art are included, they have enough display room, as in the present instance with the picture by Klee on the moss-brown rear wall. It is not hermetic isolation but generous openness which determines the mood of this room. The window wall open to the garden and the chimney wall which outlines the living area without shutting it off make this room appear much bigger than Tiffany's drawing room, which in point of fact is much more spacious.

12

13

14

14   Charles Annesley Voysey. Living room in The Orchard, Chorley Wood, 1900. In the English country-house tradition many examples emerged at an early date which were far from any imitation of the historic styles. The living room in Voysey's own house has an unmistakable personality despite its apparently simple and unobtrusive detailing. Split levels in floor and ceiling, recesses in the wall, the inclusion of the staircase, and a lively variation in the level of lighting create a rich differentiation by architectonic means, which is emphasized by the sparse furnishings.

diffusion of an exact knowledge of materials and manufacturing processes was part of its curriculum. Standardization was no longer regarded as enslavement to machinery, but on the contrary as a precondition for the free manipulation of prefabricated elements. Although the Bauhaus and its supporters in Europe, Le Corbusier in France, and the De Stijl movement in Holland, were often reproached with being dogmatic, their real message was freedom. Architectural plans were freed from domination by the façade. Advanced houses of this period are no longer given massive walls but are supported on steel or reinforced concrete stanchions. Huge windows link the interior of the house with its surroundings. Walls, freed from their load-bearing function, serve solely to divide off rooms or room areas (18). Spaciousness and brightness are the prevailing impressions conveyed by interior designs in the 1920's with their sparse furnishings and the middle of the room left free. Cabinet units which might otherwise look heavy are built into the wall. Seats of all sorts, such as the tubular steel chairs of Mart Stam and Marcel Breuer, or the famous Barcelona chair by Mies van der Rohe, have with their steel frames a weightless and transparent appearance. These rooms are not caves for shelter but instruments for the intelligent use of their inhabitants, from whom they derive their character. They are sober but humane because they serve rather than dominate. A trend toward asceticism cannot be denied, but if the ideas of modern living are to be emphasized, a certain purity of means is unavoidable.

The Bauhaus and Le Corbusier have developed a formal art of emptiness in extreme contrast to the nineteenth century which loved overflowing repletion. This concentration on a few essentials, the luxury of spaciousness, and a preference for low, narrow, rectangular furniture, recalls another, apparently remote, domestic tradition: the Japanese. In point of fact, Japan has influenced the development of Western art and architecture over the last hundred years (17). Built-in and unit furniture, as used in Japan, with individual sections let into an open frame, were already employed by English architects in the second half of the nineteenth century. A feature of the old-style Japanese house, whose framed type of structure so surprisingly recalls modern architecture, is a freely adjustable plan of the kind which Le Corbusier eloquently defends. It remains a prototype for our own times. American architects in particular continue the grid system developed in Japan from the size of the floor mats to its logical conclusion in the modular subdivision of floor and ceiling areas.

15

15   Thonet chair in the Pavillon de l'Esprit Nouveau, Paris, 1925. In the heyday of pompous reproduction furniture which was more Gothic than the Goths and more Baroque than the Baroque, chairs and easy chairs made of steam-molded wood were developed by Michael Thonet at Boppard on the Rhine. The Thonet chair was one of the main arguments in favour of functionalism. Its shape was derived from the need for strict economy – it was mass-produced by the million – and is identical with its structure. Its severe yet elegant lines and exemplary functionalism moved Le Corbusier to exhibit this veteran of modern furniture in his Pavillon de l'Esprit Nouveau at an exhibition in 1925.

The closing down of the Bauhaus in 1933 interrupted the continuity of its fruitful work, but at the same time it resulted in the world-wide diffusion of its ideas. Gropius, Mies van der Rohe, Moholy-Nagy, Herbert Bayer, Marcel Breuer, and a large number of former students and teachers emigrated to the United States. Modern domestic architecture entered upon an era of consolidation and growing influence after its revolutionary period. If the avant-garde style of the twenties was international, it was now the turn of local and national trends to come to the fore again. What has the heroic age of the modern movement bequeathed to us that is of consequence? The conditions of living will never be just a matter of dry functional analysis; and the Bauhaus regarded its task in this light. 'Beauty can only be achieved through complete harmony between technical-functional purpose and the proportions of the forms employed,' wrote Gropius. Just as one must maintain high aesthetic standards, so must one fulfill the practical requirements of a house. Whether the dining area can be reached easily from the kitchen, whether the desk of the master of the house has enough daylight, and whether the children's play corner is so arranged that the mother can keep an eye on them while she works: these points by themselves do not, in the final analysis, determine the quality of the scheme, but a sound solution will always be one that works well. Investigations into the way a

16

16 Henry van de Velde. Dining room in Count Kessler's house, Weimar, 1902–1903. While it resembled the many period styles of the nineteenth century in demanding that a room be furnished consistently in one kind of décor, Art Nouveau developed its own style which was always original and often beautiful. This dining room anticipates a number of the distinctive traits of the modern movement in the lightness of its graceful chairs, the flexibility of the layout – the dining table runs on casters – and in the easily discernible arrangement of the bright room.

house functions, which is what an appraisal of the basic principles of living entailed, produced some new and useful ideas regarding the layout of rooms. Functionalism is no less valid today than formerly, so long as it does not make dogmatic demands. The conviction, however, that we have only to ascertain the function of an object in order to determine its final shape has proved to be utopian. For the demands we make on things have themselves changed. The high stiff-backed armchair of the period of Louis XIV functioned in so far as it satisfied the Baroque love of pomp and ceremony, just as the softly upholstered, low easy chair with short armrests of the Louis XV period functioned by fulfilling the Rococo ideal of leisured ease. The formulation of the functions of a product is based upon the style of the time in exactly the same way as the invention of its shape. Our own time is not excluded from this system simply because it has made a science of functionalism.

An example of the relationship between functionalism and aesthetics is provided by the principles which have crystallized during the course of the last few decades in the matter of furniture and furnishing styles. The present situation may be complex but nonetheless certain formal categories can be recognized. The technique of deliberately exposing structural members is one. Nearly all shelf units, whether self-supporting or fixed to the wall, derive aesthetic value from the filigree-like structure of the ladders or cross-bars for the suspended shelves or cabinets. When such shelf units are erected at angles to the wall as room dividers, it is for the practical purpose of subdividing the room without destroying its unity and proportions. On the other hand, this arrangement would not be possible if its skeletal character and transparency, comparable to the steel or reinforced concrete frame in architecture, had not proved aesthetically acceptable. One of the most successful pieces of furniture of the last few decades, Harry Bertoia's easy chair, derives its decorative charm from the lattice-shaped tracery of the exposed openwork wire basket of the seat. The construction has become worthy of the shape.

These pieces have a further quality that is characteristic of the wide range of modern furniture manufacture: they are lightweight. Modern furniture is not only visually lightweight, but also literally so. This effect has been achieved by the reduction of the load-bearing parts to a few uprights and stretchers, together with the use of new materials such as steel, aluminium, plastic, and plywood. It is a quality that can be traced back to English pioneer work in the nineteenth century, but it derives mainly from the invention of new shape sin the twenties. Their lightness, and the ease with which movable pieces can be rearranged, make it possible for a room to be adapted exactly to living requirements at any given time: an effective symbol of sociological change. Formerly, a house was the home of many generations, where each piece of furniture had its designated place; now, however, the home and its furnishings change with the size of the family. The furniture of our times, easy to transport and rearrange, is planned with this in mind. Changes of layout, such as are constantly required in one-room apartments where the most varied activities take place in a small area, would otherwise be impossible.

The radical changes which transformed both architecture and the style of living so completely in the twenties, the vigorously championed and often misunderstood principles of functionalism, still have their effect on all spheres of life, but rarely cause argument now. The conceptions and shapes which were fought for then and which were advocated afresh with great enthusiasm after the Second World War, have been widely accepted today. Tubular steel chairs and tables, plastic veneers, or box-shaped furniture in the living room hardly shock anyone nowadays. They are part and parcel of our homes just like television sets, washing machines, or central heating. The modern style of furnishing is no longer the privilege of a small and exclusive group of pioneers; it is not only commercially advertised, but is also widely illustrated and endorsed in newspapers and magazines. The

17

17   Katsura Palace, Kyoto. This old Japanese house is distinguished by the art of emptiness, which achieves its effect by purity of proportions and the play of light surfaces in dark frames. The example set by Japan was all the more convincing since modern architecture with its frame construction and open plan had arrived at similar solutions. The grid system, which plays such an important part in modern buildings and décor, is nowhere more consistently and subtly employed than in the Japanese house, which is based on multiples of the dimensions of the *tatami*, or floor mat.

18 Le Corbusier. Maison La Roche, Paris, 1923. The international avant-garde – designers such as Le Corbusier in France, the architects of the De Stijl group in Rotterdam, and the Bauhaus in Germany – revolutionized our ideas of the modern house. Typical of the twenties is the pleasing relationship between flat surfaces and cubes, the everchanging play of light due to asymmetrically placed windows and top lights, and the sober surface textures: white walls, tiled floors, and the extensive renunciation of wood and textiles. The two-story living room with its galleries and staircase to the upper floor creates a new focus to which most of the house's functions are related – a changing style of daily life.

18

constant search for new shapes has not only led to intolerable abuses, it also means an almost overwhelming number of new models each year, which makes choice difficult; what is more, it often becomes impossible after a few years to duplicate a piece of furniture once considered outstanding, but now superseded by newer gimmicks. The modern orientation has become fashionable and is subjected to fashion's whims and fancies. The kidney-shaped table, the expression of ultra-modern trends after the war, is now thought to be outmoded and has been displaced. Teak furniture, still a sign of exclusive taste a few years ago, is now in every shop, and will be replaced by other kinds of wood tomorrow.

19

19 Marcel Breuer. Dining room in the Piscator residence, Berlin, 1927. The architects and designers of the twenties discovered the luxury of asceticism. The bare wall, the uniform, neutral floor covering, the few chromium-plated tubular steel chairs with their neat and precise shapes display the utmost economy of form. How dramatic the proportions can appear in this seemingly restrained style is demonstrated by the narrow band of the wall cabinet, above which three spherical lamps are symmetrically arranged.

Nowadays, the modern house is often synonymous with the fashionable house. Behind all this is the desire to 'keep up with the Jones's', to acquire certain things which one must have because they bestow definite social prestige upon their owner. When people buy a huge radio-phonograph or an ostentatious cocktail bar, or install a luxuriant plant window or enormous fireplace, this is as unlikely to be the outcome of an original idea as is that type of decoration which relies on the extensive use of bogus handmade accessories.

That this frenzied pursuit of every fashion is encouraged by the manufacturer, that this feeding of the public with examples of the type seen in movies, which bear little relation to real life, is, of course, a concomitant of the otherwise welcome emergence of the modern style. We are justified in replacing our old vacuum cleaner, radio or car by newer, more advanced models from time to time, while new curtains, covers, cushions or light-fittings can give a room a very different appearance. The value of changing our furniture to keep up with fashion is more doubtful. What is to happen to the living room suite that one saved for five years ago, and that was then the latest thing, but now no longer holds out against the critical glances of friends and neighbors? As far as comfort and quality of material are concerned, it could last decades longer, but it will have to be replaced sooner or later for a more up-to-date model. That pieces of furniture are possessions which live with us, move about with us, and eventually come to belong to us in a manner that goes beyond their actual useful value, is rarely understood in this age of speed.

Must we put up with this situation? We, too, have a period style. To recognize it amidst the great variety of products on the market today requires not only discrimination but knowledge and intelligence as well. One should know what has been accepted as valid within the modern move-ment, as for example the classical Barcelona chair of 1929 by Mies van der Rohe, which recurs as often in our examples as Eero Saarinen's saucer chair, designed in 1947 (8, 11). In the same way, the lightweight Danish chair by Arne Jacobsen (1952), available in different finishes, will stand the test of time thanks to its unobtrusive elegance. Intelligence is essential in applying this knowledge, so that the choice of furniture is adapted to one's needs and limitations, whether they be financial or architectural.

What is the shell that we have to furnish? The average home today, es-pecially in public housing projects is the three-room apartment. The size of this type of apartment has increased by approximately twenty per cent in the last ten years, but still only amounts to 750 square feet or a little over. The need for larger apartments-both in number of rooms and in the floor area of each room is constantly growing, but the rising cost of building and the corresponding rise in rents will soon impose a limit. While in some countries such as Sweden and England every effort is being made to utilize the available floor area to best advantage by careful planning, else-where ordinary apartment blocks are still marked by lack of imagination and conventional, often inadequate, standardized designs. There is not much choice under these conditions in the small apartment: one room is furnished as a bedroom, another as a child's room and the third as a living room.

Lack of space poses the problem of how to create enough storage accommo-dation for clothes, linen, and utensils while keeping as much as possible of the floor area free. It explains the growing popularity of built-in cabinets and storage walls, which have been commercially available for some time now. These units may be dismantled or added to according to need and can be taken along when moving and readily adapted to the conditions of a new apartment. The open storage wall, which accommodates not only books and objets d'art but also cupboard units for china, table linen, writing materials, or cocktail requisites, deserves its popularity.

Besides its space-saving function, it can in itself be a handsome piece and can be boldly placed to break up a large expanse of wall. Large, massive individual cabinets are less and less in demand; unit cabinets have an average width of four feet and a height of five feet. For the most part, the present popularity of light, low, rectilinear furniture can be regarded as a reaction to restricted living conditions.

Adaptation to the size of our smaller apartments can be achieved also by combining several functions in one room. A typical and well-known example is the combined living-dining room. The combined study-bedroom is becoming more popular, too, as bedroom furniture becomes more like that of the living room. The nursery is more clearly defined as a multi-purpose room in which we can distinguish the sleeping area (for two children there are often double-decker bunks), the working area (desks or working surfaces by the window), and a play area (a free space in the center of the room). The combination of kitchen and dining area or breakfast bar is equally feasible. It is quite obvious that two or more functions set new problems in furnishing a room. How can we subdivide it without spoiling the general effect? How can we avoid overcrowding when each of the different zones needs a definite minimum of furniture? Which solutions provide a practical layout with the minimum friction, for example, in the matter of circulation, and how do they affect the over-all impression created by the room? All these are problems for which no standard solution can be postulated, as many acceptable schemes are often contradicted by others which are no less satisfactory aesthetically.

The multi-purpose room is, however, by no means limited to the small apartment. The combined living-dining room in particular can be found in more spacious apartments and in private houses, where there are fewer restrictions of space. Thus we see that combination of different functions in one room does not stem from practical considerations alone. It is determined by a conception of living which advocates the large, amply dimensioned general-purpose room in preference to a series of small but varied cells. This idea is applied most frequently in Scandinavian and American houses built on the open-plan system. Dividing walls between different zones are eliminated, and the living area, dining alcove, study, and kitchen, and occasionally the nursery and bedroom also, are brought into a continuous spatial relationship. Recesses, narrow passages, partition walls projecting into the room, split levels, or lowered ceilings accentuate the separate areas architecturally without disrupting the continuity of the rooms. Variety and contrast are used to mark off one area from another: dark is set against light; solid walls are broken by expanses of plate glass; rough plaster contrasts with smooth wood paneling. As simple a device as a slight change in color scheme can differentiate parts of a room. Any particular zone, for example the dining area, can be divided off by means of folding partitions, sliding doors, or curtains.

Behind this growing trend toward the open plan, apart from the aesthetic ideal of spaciousness, lies our much more informal way of living and the constant lack of servants; both are reasons for making a simple, labor-saving, and easilyrun household desirable. Close family coexistence is an important assumption in these circumstances, for the open plan not only entails greater freedom but also imposes upon each person the duty of consideration for others. The open plan idea is steadily gaining in popularity, not least in cooperative arpartments where the owner can determine the layout or in cases where spacious old apartment blocks are rebuilt and can be transformed by taking out partition walls. The private house, however, offers the best opportunities. By allowing certain rooms to continue through one and a half or two storys, we are afforded a delightful surprise by the change in ceiling height; what is more, a further effect is achieved by the view from the gallery which is usually built into such high and extensive living rooms.

Whether the size of a dwelling is generous or limited, whether it is a spacious private house, a small apartment, or a many-cornered attic flat, the

20

impression the rooms make is largely determined by the extent to which they reflect the personality of the occupants and how well they have succeeded in giving the dwelling an individual character by creating a living atmosphere that is immediately perceptible on entering. This atmosphere may depend on a carefully considered but unobtrusive harmony of colors and shapes, or equally on a play of contrasts, the combination of antique and modern furniture, or on the particular stress laid on a certain area by special lighting or the work of art that it features. Sometimes it is less the furniture, carpets, curtains, or lamps than the small personal additions which give the room its individuality: an inherited chest, old toys, a valuable clock, a Sicilian jug, or a Malayan *kris* brought home from one's travels – in short, those items which have no practical function but to which we are attached. Such items are not relics or exhibition pieces. They don't require a formal setting but should look as casual and unrehearsed as when we saw them for the first time in the odd corner of an antique shop or on a journey.

Since the Werkbund and Bauhaus, modern furniture is no longer ornamented. Ornament and décor are confined to upholstery, carpets, and curtains, but these too are often chosen in a plain, unpatterned fabric. These practical but pretty things occupy the space that was formerly reserved for ornaments. Modern houses, whose furniture has a consistently rectilinear character, tend to be somewhat ascetic and harsh. What chance and personal taste have added softens the dogmatic quality which is peculiar to such homes without detracting from their clarity of line. On the contrary, the clear-cut silhouette of a chest of drawers or a plastic-topped table will often gain in significance when contrasted with the irregular and lively shape of an old candlestick. It is not, however, the aesthetic charm of such shapes that is important, but the personal value that we ourselves attach to them.

The desire for contemporary living should never be a convention; it must allow scope for individual tastes. We should not be afraid now and again to break the strict rules laid down by unwavering partisans of the modern movement against what is called *kitsch* (roughly equivalent to 'corny'). Only mass-produced ornaments which try to imitate the appearance of real craftwork have no claim to mercy.

'Modern living' does not mean living exclusively with modern furniture. Anything of quality fits in, no matter from what epoch it dates. The possibilities range from subtle differentiation to strong contrasts. The furniture of our time is comparable in its lightness and structural elegance to that of the Biedermeier period, and yet with Rococo too; elements which are so related permit some fine nuances to be achieved in combination. Pronounced contrasts have their aesthetic justification as well. The juxtaposition of a divan designed by Le Corbusier in tubular steel and leather with a painted peasant cupboard shows up even more clearly the individuality of both pieces. In such ensembles, unlike the room completely furnished in an antique style, no attempt is made to conjure up the illusion of a bygone age. Each item exists in its own right without disturbing the others; the piece of antique furniture may be regarded as a quotation, contributing to the whole composition the charm of nonconformity.

In the years of development between the two World Wars, a new code was framed for the choice and use of materials, which introduced into our homes a number of unusual substances previously reserved exclusively for industry. Since then concrete and steel, glass and plastics have become more familiar and are taken for granted as mediums for interior decoration. Designers are constantly seeking to add to their attractiveness, while endeavoring at the same time to enliven their inert coldness by employing natural materials: rough-hewn stone blocks and bricks for walls; ceramic

21

21 The open plan in a two-story living room, where the ceiling slopes down toward the window. Furniture arrangement is determined by the architectural frame: the sitting area is in the front near the window in the spacious, sunny part of the room; below the gallery are the desk and library, set apart from the main room, with an intimate character achieved through the presence of a low beamed ceiling and warm timber and fabric textures. Situated on the gallery, open to the sleeping quarters on the left, is the study, roofed by a boarded ceiling, like a tent.

22

22   Old and new do not exclude each other but can reciprocally heighten their effectiveness. In this American foyer, nineteenth century furniture and accessories – the sideboard, wall clock and rocking chair – are contrasted with the other furniture with its angular chromium-plated steel frames. Apart from the soft, curved, plastic shape of the leather chairs, line and silhouette predominate. The light tiles and the rough, whitewashed brick wall show up the contours of the dark wood; the curves of the bentwood chair contribute as much to the overall effect of the group as the foliage of the fan-palm.

tiles and stone slabs for the floor; timber as a lining for walls or ceilings, in exposed beam construction, in the form of planks or boards. What we need is the living quality of something that has grown naturally, not simply in order to use it as a romantic backdrop, but to contrast with the products of our technical world. As in modern furniture the functional and technological harmonize with the organic and plastic, the style may be elaborated or modified by variations in surface textures.

New technical processes are continually modifying developments. The use of fiberglass and plastics, for example, makes it possible to create furniture of startling shapes with equally novel external finishes. Plastic laminates in lieu of wood veneers give a new surface interest to furniture. Unusual structural effects in tables and bookcases are achieved by the use of enameled, oxidized, and chromium-plated metal frames. Together with these, natural materials are employed to provide textural interest: wicker-work of rattan and split cane, or covers of natural or black leather, and of course the most varied rare woods, which have been employed more and more frequently in recent years (25). Attractive materials and textures play an important part in the treatment of large areas. This applies to wallpapers, paintwork, or plaster, curtains, carpets, and upholstery. Textiles offer countless possibilities, while textural contrasts add excitement to the room or create a background that sets off the furniture.

The choice of color in interiors poses one of the most difficult problems. Colors exert a decisive effect upon a room, especially as their influence cannot easily be controlled. One badly chosen shade can spoil a carefully planned color scheme; a color range which happens to appeal to the taste and temperament of the occupants can completely ruin a room's proportions. The uneasiness which we sometimes feel in a room, without being able to explain why – a sensation of unrest or coldness, of oppression or agoraphobia – has its origin only too often in the wrong choice of color. The effect of color in the home can be judged from two different angles. First there is its psychological effect. Warm colors are stimulating: red energetic and active, yellow gay, orange vital. Green is refreshing without being aggressive. Cool and distant colors include turquoise and most shades

23

23 In this French example, the contrast between the sturdy peasant table and the rest of the modern furniture has been toned down rather than emphasized by the soft carpet and the upholstery. The compact and solid table provides the essential counterpoint to the otherwise unexciting atmosphere of the ensemble.

of blue. The 'temperature' of a room can in this way be changed by colors. Cold colors cool a sunny room with a southern prospect, while red shades warm a cold room facing north. But none of these color values are absolute. They change as soon as another color is added or as the light changes, and they do not affect everyone with the same intensity.

First of all, complementary colors can be used together: purple and green, orange and ultramarine, crimson and blue-green, blue-violet and yellow. In these combinations, one color should dominate and the other serve only as a contrast, otherwise the effect is too garish. Which color dominates depends on the extent of the areas involved, or on the intensity of the color. An easy chair in brilliant red can look more intensely colorful than a whole carpet in a darker or paler green.

Many more combinations are possible when unifying colors having little intensity of their own are employed. The so-called non-colors, black, white, and gray, can be recommended; they make even unusual color contrasts harmonize. Here, too, the risk is greater the larger the area on which bright colors have been used. In doubtful cases, carpets or curtains should be restrained rather than strong; a gray floor, for example, or a natural wool carpet will intensify the brilliance of the remaining colors in the room. The non-colors, which are not meant to compete with the other colors, possess the property of intensifying them. A blue, red, or yellow on a black, gray, or white background appears more brilliant than it would on a colored background. Gray has the additional peculiarity of accentuating shapes. A beautifully contoured sculpture or vase will be all the more effective against a gray background.

Monochrome schemes of closely related colors are among the most difficult artistic achievements of color manipulation. Interiors in different shades of yellow – lemon, acid, and mustard yellow – or in related shades like red, purple, and pink can look attractive frequently but misfire just as often. Above all, we must remember that the psychological effect of closely related colors is similar and is therefore intensified in such combinations. Nobody can bear to be in a room for long if its color is perpetually chilling or else over-stimulating. For rooms in constant use, therefore, such solutions are generally inappropriate.

Besides the psychological effect of colors, certain architectural considerations must be borne in mind. Colors not only transmit definite moods, they also provide different spatial effects. The human eye is accustomed out-of-doors to connect cool blues and violets with distance and warm earthy tones with proximity. The hazy horizon appears blue and violet, while nearby things that can be touched seem warm: the earthy brown of a footpath, the golden orange of a cornfield, the vermilion of an adjacent roof. These spatial properties are attributed to the colors as permanent qualities by the optics of the eye. When we furnish our home we can make use of this. If a room is too high and needs correcting by optical means, a warm color should be used on the ceiling instead of white, which is spatially neutral. If a room is too long and narrow, the far wall can be brought forward by painting it rust or burnt orange. Conversely, if a short room needs extending, a cool blue can be used to make an oppressive wall appear distant.

These effects can be intensified by corresponding patterns in the wallpaper. The psychological and spatial values of color provide the most reliable pointers for the color scheme of a room. But here, too, style and fashion – difficult to separate – play their part. The light yellow of the Napoleonic era which went so well with the clear-cut contours of Empire-style furniture, belonged without any doubt to the manner of the period around 1800. Do the blue-green shades which so often occur in our furnishing fabrics, especially where Scandinavian teak furniture is concerned, belong as indissolubly to our contemporary interiors? Essentially fashionable colors such as purple, which has enjoyed the favor of couturiers and interior decorators for the last five years, should be used only for easily exchangeable accessories such as cushions, tablecloths, or small rugs, and not for the more costly

24

24 Elegance of form and clever harmony of textures are the marks of distinction in this room: the material warmth of the pastel gray carpet, for example, against the smoothness of the chalice-shaped chairs and the white plastic cabinet doors; the coolness of the strongly veined marble slab against the silky warm tone of the teak. The fine-grained surface of a painted wall serves as a background.

25

25 The texture of natural materials – long bricks with white joints and narrow pine boarding – give the room warmth and liveliness; note in addition the large glass end wall and the differing materials of the carpet and upholstery, the wickerwork of the cane chair, and the smoothness of the leather cushions on the chimney seat. Altogether an ensemble whose effectiveness results mainly from the close harmony of different materials.

larger pieces of furniture. The popularity of intense and bright colors which are hardly toned down at all and stand out clearly as color accents derives from the style of our time. The dark tones of the end of the nineteenth century, the dusty colors and Rembrandtesque shadows that weighed so heavily on interiors, led to open opposition for the first time in the emergence of Art Nouveau, a protest whose results are still valid for us today although the individual colors may have changed.

The greater abundance of light entering by broad windows and room-high glass doors is in keeping with the trend toward brighter colors. As regards artificial light, chandeliers in the center of the ceiling are only appropriate in imposing symmetrical rooms, and make no sense unless a central light fixture has to illuminate a large table in the middle. In rooms divided into several equally important functional centers the obvious thing is to provide each zone with its own light: hanging lamps over the occasional table in the sitting area or above the writing desk, standard lamps, which have an advantage over table lamps in that they take up no table space, or wall lights. Unfortunately the latter tend to combine slight practical value with a susceptibility to trumpery design. Artificial light is no longer used without regard to the purpose and layout of a room but constitutes a part of its decorative scheme.

We have seen that choice of color can correct the proportions of a room; careful attention to the lighting can have the same effect. In a room that has even general lighting or is lit from the center, no strong spatial effect is achieved. Division into areas of light and shade helps to articulate a room; the greater the contrast between light and dark, the stronger will be the feeling of protection in the light zone. Light enlarges a room: a low ceiling illuminated by lamps appears higher in the reflected light. A long room can be considerably shortened by points of light situated two-thirds of the way along the depth of the room, or by lamps arranged diagonally.

Light is an irrational element in the home. From the subtle lighting fantasies of American homes to the easily installed spotlights that can illuminate a picture or a particularly beautiful collector's piece, light provides innumerable opportunities for giving free rein to the imagination. Invisible striplights behind a cornice not only afford shadow-free illumination, for example over a bookcase, where uniform light is desirable, but can also transform a wall or ceiling into something intangible.

The hall

27 The hall is the vestibule to the whole house. This Italian entrance hall gives one an immediate idea of the general atmosphere of the house: the carefully thought-out display of a few painstakingly chosen objects, ascetic luxury, delicately harmonizing tones giving a free hand to the introduction of works of art. The purple cushion that harmonizes with the wine-red of the door, shelf, and chair cover makes an improvised seat on the steps for long telephone conversations.

The hall

The order of importance in which we think of the rooms in our home often places the entrance hall last — a less paradoxical fact, for everyone acknowledges the importance of making a good first impression. It is in the hall that we receive our guests, and it is here that we ourselves wish to feel at home on our arrival. That is why we should devote particular care and attention to the appearance of the hall.

No other room can be so varied and different. The scale ranges from the tiny lobby to the imposing vestibule, from the windowless room to the sundrenched conservatory. There can be no one universal solution to furnishing a hall, and indeed the same applies to any other room. Finally, it is particularly important in this instance to pay attention to the specific spatial proportions involved.

Equally important is the function of a hall. First of all it has a practical purpose; it supplies the means of communication from the outside to any number of connecting rooms. There will usually be several doors in a minimum of wall space. The internal traffic from room to room obliges us to keep the center of the hall as free as possible. And yet the hall should have an atmosphere of its own and should be inviting for guests and the people living in the house, besides serving as a means of transition to the other rooms.

Brightness and color are all-important. If no direct daylight can enter, wall and ceiling lamps should give a diffuse light, warm and not dazzling, which illuminates the room evenly. Walls, ceiling and floor should also be light and pleasant. The idea of experimenting with strong colors and striking wallpapers in the hall is generally not a happy one. That does not mean, however, that we must forego lively patterns and strong colors entirely. Often, one single wall with a patterned paper or a photo-mural makes a vivid impression (45), and wallpaper or a strong color is frequently required to camouflage unsuitable proportions. Horizontal stripes widen a narrow wall; a strong color foreshortens distance; a dark-painted ceiling imparts the optical illusion that it is lower. The floor, too, should be bright. Often sand-colored stone slabs are used. A plastic covering or a tiled floor creates a pleasant effect and stands up well under constant hard wear.

Since the days of our grandparents, hall furniture has undergone a complete transformation. Heavy wardrobes, which often turned the hall into a dark lumber room, have been replaced by lightweight furniture; the ornate stand and the cast-iron umbrella rack have been discarded in favor of simpler items. A shelf for scarves, gloves, and bags, a mirror, a few coat hooks, and an umbrella-stand are the essentials. If there is room for more, a low set of shelves, a cabinet, or a small chest of drawers can replace the single shelf, and there will then be room for keys, brushes, sunglasses, magazines, and numerous other items. A large mirror adds considerably to the apparent size of the room. The stand should neatly combine hatrack, hooks, shelves, mirror, and umbrella stands in one unit (30). This arrangement has two advantages over coat hooks alone: it prevents damage to the wall behind from scratches or stains and also provides hooks at different heights, so that children can hang up their hats and coats without help. If the telephone is also in the hall, where it can be reached most easily from all the other rooms, a small cupboard unit may be provided, with telephone directory, notepad, ashtray, and preferably a seat as well.

Large halls can, and often must, be furnished more fully. A fine chest, an old grandfather clock, an antique cupboard, or a bookshelf can be featured against wall areas; a small group of chairs or a stand at angles to the wall can divide it up. Here, too, is the place for a built-in closet wall which, besides holding coats and hats, can accommodate all those things for which there is no room in the bedroom, living room, or kitchen (37). Built-in cabinets flanking a door or window can often improve the proportions of a hall.

The most spacious type of hall, the imposing foyer, is for the most part to be found in big detached houses. Here the staircase to the upper floor is often a major feature in two-story buildings. It should thus be carefully designed to fit into the architectural frame (52–55). The hall is incorporated into the sequence of the living rooms and is often supplemented by a separate cloakroom and a bathroom (41, 42). The hall is also a good place for pictures and objets d'art.

Anyone entering a house or apartment wants to shed his hat, coat, umbrella, bag, and gloves. A few hooks and a shelf on the wall help, but are really very casual and improvised. A complete unit with shelves and hooks has many practical advantages: the wallpaper or paint is protected from damp and scratches. The simplest and cheapest of these units (28) does without a hatrack and provides a stool to put things on. Between this example and the complete hall stand (30) many variations are possible. In any case, with a little imagination and skill, it is not difficult to create an eye-catching feature from some necessary item of furniture.

28   A variant of the popular hall stand made of coarse or fine steel mesh. Thin crossbars on a metal frame are fitted with plastic-covered coat hooks at a chosen height. The die-shaped stool, with a frame made of the same square steel tubing as the hall stand, and the simple telephone unit achieve a stylish result.

29   This stand in an apartment in Milan features walnut slats in front of a blue linen panel. The adjustable hooks are of black enameled steel. A shelf for bags, scarves, and hats, and a ceramic vase for umbrellas complete the unit.

30   This stand, combining shelves, mirror, hooks, and umbrella rack, is attached to the wall by three metal rails. Crossbars are screwed on at different levels and these are fitted with coat hooks that can be moved sideways. The unframed mirror, the pressed-steel glove compartment, and the umbrella-stand, on the right, are in exactly correct proportion to one another.

28

30

29

31

32

33

31, 32   One wall of this hall is fitted with a large mirror almost up to the ceiling, providing an optical extension to the room, which is only 54 square feet in area. Below the mirror is a shelf for the telephone, hats, and gloves; from it two drawers are suspended. A coat rail and shelf are fitted into the recess opposite. Its back wall is covered with the same material as the curtains. The room is amply lit by windows on either side of the door. Two strip lights, which run behind a molding above the mirror and coat rail, provide diffuse but bright illumination at night. Ceiling and walls appear light against the dark stone slabs of the floor and the vividly patterned material lining the recess. The umbrella stand decorated with color photographs is an amusing idea.

33   The square slabs of the floor form an effective contrast to the strip paneling, which is used as a wall covering and is also painted on the door and the wall visible in the mirror. The quiet repetition of vertical and horizontal lines gives the room a unified and intimate atmosphere that is further emphasized by concealed lighting above the coat space. The hatshelf is of glass so that the recess is fully illuminated and visually undivided. The rectilinear pattern of stone slabs and timber is repeated by the design of the coat recess.

34–36 The hall in this family house in Munich is less for show than for use. The problem was to provide plenty of storage space to house clothes, shoes, suitcases, tools, and bulky domestic and sports equipment. The two walls to the right and left of the entrance door were therefore utilized to the last inch. Adjustable shelves and drawers of different heights hold the wide variety of objects. Solid cabinet doors would have seemed too heavy and confining. Slatted doors that run on rails at the top and casters below hide shelves and drawers elegantly and inexpensively. For the family, the hall cabinets are easily accessible, while the visitor, upon entering, sees a gaily detailed room whose light woodwork and red tiled floor create an agreeable atmosphere.

34

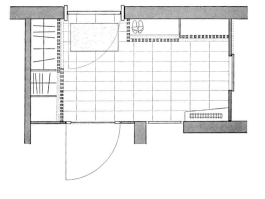

35

36

In modern apartments or small single-story houses there is often insufficient storage space or even none at all. Where should one put the vases, the Christmas decorations, the electric train set, the spare bedding, and the unused winter or summer clothes? If the hall is not too small and has sufficient wall space, solutions are always possible. People who live in rented apartments can buy cabinet units that later can be taken apart and re-assembled elsewhere (40). Those who own their homes may install slatted doors in front of shelves quite inexpensively (34–36), or build closets (39) and whole walls of cabinets (37, 38). Usually the amount of storage space created by such additions justifies their cost. As built-in fittings must nearly always be individually made, the subdivisions can also be designed for specific requirements.

37

38

37, 38 This built-in closet spans the hall and divides it from the living room. The double cabinet on the left serves as a wardrobe. Its frequent use has dictated the installation of folding doors that project only eight inches into the room. The two doors and the flap of the small compartment on the far left are fitted with mirrors. All three parts can be opened by wooden handles. The square compartment and the inside face of the flap, on which handbags may be placed, are covered with plastic. Stripping separates the cabinet wall from the ceiling and floor.

39

40

39   The grained wooden wall and the tiled floor with its white seams give
this hall a rustic appearance that goes well with the dining-room furniture.
The Peasant Baroque gilt mirror fits in harmoniously. The apparently continuous boarding of the panels almost completely conceals two cabinets built
into the depth of the walls and preserves a unified appearance.

40   Much thought has been given to the divisions in this cupboard which,
with its depth of only one foot, can be accommodated in even a small hall.
Two compartments with varnished sliding doors provide coat space; adjustable glass shelves with cut-out hand-holds accommodate all the small items;
the telephone is placed high enough to be out of children's reach; a ventilated compartment holds shoes. The natural wood presents a neutral
appearance, leaving a free choice of colors in wallpaper, carpet, and curtains.

41, 42   Beyond its purely practical purpose, the hall conditions the guest to the atmosphere of the house. In the two examples illustrated here, this is done by the matter-of-course coexistence of modern architectural detail – a strip of glass round the door (41), for example, or a glass-brick wall and antique furniture (42). Both rooms are flooded with light. The warm color of the wood creates a pleasant, inviting atmosphere. The furniture looks effective in front of the light, monochrome walls, and the glass bricks create a striking silhouette effect. Sparsely distributed collector's pieces stress the feeling of special quality and in each case the chest with a mirror or picture above it stands opposite a feature on the other wall: a marble table with a graceful candlestick (41), a slate slab with a petrified water lily (42).

41

42

The heavy oak bookcase with its glass doors and window curtains belongs to the past. In its place we find the open bookshelf. There is not always enough space in the living room for a book wall, while shelves in the study and bedroom often hold only necessities. In the hall or passage, however, we usually have a long wall where a library can be housed. Colorful book spines and the interplay of tall and short, thick and thin volumes create a pattern more individual than any wallpaper design or colored curtain.

In the example below (43), indoors and out, the worlds of books and of nature have been brought together with sure discernment. The continuous lines of the shelves and the placing of a small sofa along the wall stress the direction of the comparatively small room toward the plate-glass window, with the flywheel of an old steam engine closing the vista.

43

44

45

44   The tall, narrow, tunnel-like hall in old-fashioned apartment houses is the stumblingblock of every interior decorator. There is rarely enough room for chairs, and a chest of drawers or cabinet is not enough to subdivide the overlong wall. In this case, the problem of the narrow 'canyon' has been solved by means of shelves for books and objets d'art. The black background lends an impression of greater width and the free wall spaces are enlivened by delicate architectural outlines. The wooden struts run from floor to ceiling; the solid shelves are adjustable and are kept in place by little metal clips. The ceiling appears lower than it is thanks to a coat of colored paint, but the hanging lamp and the narrow strip of carpet on the floor tend to emphasize the height and length of the room.

45   In this Italian example the hall has become an eleg: reception room. The main feature is the decorated wall wit photo-mural of part of a fresco by Piero della Francesca. T graphic effect of this black-and-white photograph is balanc by the color accents of the books, which are placed agains dark background on smoked glass shelves. The ceiling is a painted dark. The technique of contrasts has been carried c to the last detail: the mural, which is light at the top, has be finished with a black cornice molding, while the dark w behind the books has been enclosed by white moldings. T light marble slabs of the floor add to the room's elegance.

46

47

46, 47   If the entrance door is on the long wall, it is possible in spacious halls to separate the main door from storage areas by a room-divider. In example 46, an Italian hall, this is a mat made of Japanese reeds attached to wooden slats; while in example 47, a German one, it is a screen of horizontal boards. The entrance in both has been left bare to focus attention on one main feature: the group formed by the plant and the blackamoor in the Italian example, and the floor vase reflected in the mirror in the German one. In both halls the character of the room has been greatly influenced by the stone floor. In the upper illustration there are some particularly beautiful marble slabs, while the lower one shows a floor paved with natural stone in varying shapes and colors.

48

49

50

Every fashion expert knows that it is the small items, the accessories, which are decisive in the success of a model. This rule also applies to the accessories that can be used in a hall. Even the humblest ante room can be enhanced by a beautiful mirror, a charming wall decoration, or a distinctive choice of color that gives it style. It should be remembered, however, that just as in fashion, not too many clever ideas should be strung together, or at least that they should form a harmonious ensemble.

48, 49   After the closet a mirror and shelf are the most important items in furnishing a hall. They are decorative as well as practical and may be placed in a variety of ways: set on a flat wall or recessed in an alcove, hung symmetrically or arranged in striking imbalance. The narrow shelf fixed to the wall by brackets and the simply framed round mirror (48) provide an effective feature. The Rococo frame of the mirror in example 49 has been placed against a piece of black velveto. It is set off by a simple shelf.

50   A practical arrangement for telephone conversations. Next to the leather cushion on the bench is a small open cupboard unit for the telephone directories. Its top is a writing surface.

51

51   A bench with a teak drawer unit on the left and a square mirror in a natural wood
frame, hung slightly off center, form a composition in the hall. The severity of rectilinear
surfaces and cubes is softened by the mushroom-shaped lamp and the curves of the chair.

52

The shape of a staircase can influence radically the whole impression made by the hall. While the staircase formerly filled the room with its solid weight, modern technical developments make it possible to give it the appearance of filigree. By using a scaffolding of steel tubing as a support for lightweight board steps, one can incorporate a staircase into a hall without crowding it visually. The rhythm of open treads is a dominant feature which makes it necessary to choose furnishings in harmony with this theme.

53

52   Access to an upper landing had to be provided here from a comparatively small floor area. The open board stairs form a strong silhouette against the big glass wall. Both lower and upper landings are carried by a pair of tubular steel columns. A large potted plant and a grandfather clock are featured in the room and emphasize the different planes of the staircase.

53   The simplest and at the same time the most elegant solution can be seen in this Danish terrace house, where the staircase was reduced to a series of treads cantilevered from a central beam. The top lighting reveals the structural significance of the design. Note the remarkable cantilevered handrail: it is fixed only at the top and runs unsupported for the whole length of the staircase.

54

55

54 This open staircase, placed above the entrance steps in front of a glass-brick wall, fits into the smallest amount of space and also permits diffused daylight to flood the hall. The treads are fixed to a stringer on the outside and to round iron bars and steel brackets on the hall side. The staircase area is outlined in brick. The tall mirror accentuates the landing and makes the room look wider.

55 A scaffold of tubular steel rectangles supports the treads, which are fixed to the wall on the other side. Above, a light glazed with Plexiglass has been let into the ceiling.

The living-room

56 The colored illustration opposite is described on page 79

The living room

The living room is the center of every home and the background for most amily activities. Here the family gathers to talk, read, work, or play, and here also they entertain their friends. The room has thus a twofold purpose. The private and the social spheres meet here, whereas in our grandparents' time they were still divided between at least two rooms. Life today is less formal, less determined by convention, and the problems of furnishing are different. No matter how one decides to furnish the living room, with elegance or with casual comfort, in a sophisticated or a rustic style, it is here that one's personal tastes and manner of living are most clearly manifested. The surest way to a sensible and aesthetically satisfying solution is to determine the functions of the living room and then decide what furniture is needed to fulfill them. The sitting group composed of couch, easy chairs, and coffee table is the essential unit. Next one can add cupboard units, chests, and cabinets for general storage. The objects kept in open shelves and bookcases – objets d'art, books, china, and collector's pieces – must be considered part of the décor, for they help create the personality of a room. If a desk or working surface is needed in the living room, this can be incorporated in the storage wall or, if natural daylight is essential, it may be located by a window. Radio, record player, and television set can be incorporated into an interestingly subdivided wall unit and need not conceal their technical appearance. A play corner merits consideration, even in homes where there is a nursery, for children should occasionally join the grown-ups.

The special atmosphere that a living room can radiate does not depend on the choice of furniture alone, but on such things as an interesting relationship between the different parts. Often variation in the color of the walls or two different carpets are enough to create a visual separation between the various parts of the living room. Pieces of furniture like bookcases, sofas, or low chests placed at angles to the room can also divide it up. Often – especially in new buildings – the ground plan contains irregularities which can be exploited.

One can easily set apart a desk, a reading corner, or a group of chairs around a radio or television set in an alcove.

In the detached house there may be projecting chimneys, roof beams, or split

57

levels to divide up the room. The sunken recess or 'conversation pit', which
has recently gained widespread popularity in the United States, and the
two- or one-and-a-half-story living room, provide further stimulating ideas
for room dividers.

Lighting, too, is being increasingly used nowadays to articulate a room by
equipping each zone with its own sources of illumination. The conventional
light in the middle of the ceiling is dispensed with more and more frequently.
For small rooms a standard lamp and wall lights often suffice. Writing
surfaces must, of course, have their own good light. Where the ceiling has
only one electric outlet, as is the case in many rented apartments, the
cord can be led along and suspended from a hook wherever light is required.
The visible cord need not be ugly, for it has a certain graphic charm of its own.
The lamp can be suspended very low over a casual table to concentrate the
light on the sitting area. This solution is particularly suitable in conditions
of limited space where even a standard lamp would be in the way. Larger
wall and ceiling areas are best lit by adjustable lamps, which can either be

used to spotlight pictures and objects or else be directed toward the wall to provide diffuse illumination by reflection. An interesting effect is achieved by concealed strip lights fixed behind a curtain or a cornice: the great flood of light thus achieved can soften the solidity of a wall or even dematerialize it. Modern architecture creates a new relationship between indoors and out, between house and garden. It is comparatively easy to establish this connection in a detached house: broad glass walls and French windows lead from the house into the garden, bring into the room the changing patterns of daylight and the rhythm of the four seasons. In a more limited way, these tendencies also apply to the apartment. Windows have become larger everywhere; many new apartments have balconies with flower boxes and greenery. The plant window has become so well established that we need only add this about it: where it involves a real connection with plants and flowers, it creates a relationship with nature that tenants in an apartment house must usually do without.

Sloping ceilings and the consciously emphasized textural qualities of materials such as wood and stone have been exploited to varying effects. The generous width of one room (57) has been accentuated by the unusual wood-veneered ceiling which rises towards the window wall on the right. In the second example (58) the ceiling slopes down towards the window walls and enhances the intimate coziness of the room. The narrow ceiling boards vary greatly in color and grain and avoid emphasizing the length of the room.

57 The furniture arrangement here, without being forced into one particular layout, depends on the large fireplace. Rough-hewn stone has been used not only in the fireplace, but for the plant trough behind it that continues onto the balcony, and for the parapet wall of the terrace. The irregular veining of the masonry contrasts with the tile pattern of the floor finish.

58 The room receives daylight from a gable wall not visible in this picture and from a window on the right of the fireplace, which lights up the timber-lined sitting area. The dining table on the right is easily served by a hatch from the kitchen. Slender steel beams contribute to an impression of sophisticated simplicity, which the room conveys despite tis rustic materials.

58

59

60

or and fabric quality have become such essential mediums
xpression in interior decoration that they indicate personal
e as much as the shape and arrangement of the furniture it-
   Whether you are inclined toward strong contrasts or
er pastel effects, there are certain rules in either case which
 to save disappointment later on. Thus it is advisable to
ct textiles in restrained shades for large areas like carpets,
ains, and sofa covers. Movable and replaceable objects such
shions, flower vases, and wall decorations can, however, be
ngly contrasting. Further effects may also be achieved by
ly varying materials: wood in combination with chromium-
ed or enameled steel tubing, cool marble slabs or trans-
nt glass above soft carpets, shaggy textiles and furs next to
oth linens.

The dark gray shades of couch and carpet, together with
white storage wall, combine to provide the background for

a few strong color contrasts: a blue and a red easy chair and the
colored book spines. Even the choice of flowers was carefully
adapted to these colors.

60   A room that derives its impression of light and space not
only from its delicate, pale colors, but also from the arrangement of rows of low bench-type seats and wall cabinets along
its periphery. The upper wall areas and the center of the room
are thus largely empty. Two easy chairs can turn this sitting
area into a circle.

61   Restrained basic tones in gray and brown, soft warm
textiles such as the shaggy pile carpet, and the fur rug on the stool,
and the wooden table top lend an air of intimacy to this sitting
area. The colors of the movable objects, the friezelike painting,
cushions, and flowers have been lovingly chosen to harmonize
with each other.

62

63

ether the living-room furniture is bought as a suite or
 units acquired singly, certain basic pieces are essential,
 nely a couch, two easy chairs, and a table. This combination
 rds an opportunity for family relaxation and leisure while
 ving the needs of social life, for it can easily seat five people.
 e largest number of seats may be arranged in the smallest
 a by the use of bench seating, often turning corners. If, how-
 r, a divan has to go in the living room, the problem arises of
 w to provide a back to lean against when sitting. A certain
 ount of comfort is often sacrificed (62, 63) in favor of an
 thetically pleasing solution. How these simple elements,
 plemented by small personal additions, can achieve com-
 tely different spatial effects in a relatively small area, is shown
 the examples on these two pages.

The simple wooden divan with its dark upholstery is the
 ter of gravity in this sitting-room group, supplemented by
 o cane easy chairs and a table with a white plastic top. A
 ored carpet on a plain deal floor and the particularly engaging

corner near the window (the small oil painting hangs in front
of a curtain) give this room its warm, serene, and feminine
charm.

63   Chromium-plated steel frames, light-colored leather, and
the opaque glass table top lend a restrained, almost cool
character to the furniture of this small living room on a Danish
housing estate. The divan at right angles clearly divides off the
living area of the room. The stove and fur rug, the light woolen
curtains, and the spherical Japanese paper lantern provide warm
accents.

64   This sitting area in a Finnish living room is dominated by a
right-angled bench seat whose dark upholstery stands out
against the whitewashed wall. Two lightweight easy chairs of
bleached canework mark off the sitting area in front of the long
coffee table without isolating it from the rest of the room. The
bookshelves below the ceiling – preferably not for books in
frequent use – emphasize the enclosing character of the alcove.

65

66

65, 66 In this long, narrow living room, the sitting area is grouped around the old tiled stove, which has been rebuilt as a fireplace. Easy chairs with light covers, a glass-topped table on a deep yellow carpet, and mountains of bright cushions along the wall provide the dominant effects in the room. Coexistence of many different elements – the television set on the shelf below a collection of Orrefors glass, or an abstract painting next to the flowered Delft tiles of the fireplace – produces a harmonious whole. The length of the room is divided by a straw mat suspended from the ceiling partitioning off the dining area. This room divider and the curtains by the plant window (66) are illuminated by floor reflectors; they thereby become walls of light, which help detract from the unsatisfactory proportions of the room.

67, 68 In this roomy flat of an apartment block in Milan, a large room was available but of a very angular plan. One of its alcoves was just right as a sitting area. The installation of an old stove added depth to the alcove and a vivid decorative note to the entire room. On the back wall is a bookshelf with a bench underneath to provide more seats. Comfortable upholstered furniture, mostly in bright red, lends the alcove a certain coziness and stresses that this is a place of leisure and conversation. The front of the room remains uncluttered with its long, narrow table and its elegant lightweight chairs (68). The character of the room is greatly influenced by the warm timber colors of the floor and the close-boarded ceiling which spans the room like a tent; between these run the white walls with their lively angles.

67

68

The furnishing of old flats with irregularly shaped rooms often poses difficult problems: how can a living center be created in a long tunnel-like room, and how can alcoves and wall projections be utilized? With imagination and a gift for improvisation one can make a virtue of necessity. These two examples from very disparate zones – Sweden and Italy – with all their diversity of detail, reveal a sure hand in the combination of different elements.

69 A high, severe room with refined furnishings recalling Oriental models. The sunken conversation center and the chimney wall are faced with travertine slabs. The light velour carpet serves as a background to the dark upholstery, the Oriental rug, and the two cane seats. This static and elegant ensemble is supplemented by generous plant arrangements and valuable collector's pieces. Concealed lights behind a glass panel at the left illuminate the floor.

70

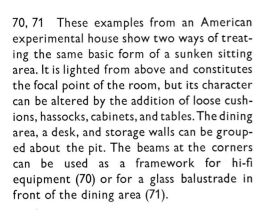

70, 71 These examples from an American experimental house show two ways of treating the same basic form of a sunken sitting area. It is lighted from above and constitutes the focal point of the room, but its character can be altered by the addition of loose cushions, hassocks, cabinets, and tables. The dining area, a desk, and storage walls can be grouped about the pit. The beams at the corners can be used as a framework for hi-fi equipment (70) or for a glass balustrade in front of the dining area (71).

71

An idea for a new shape in sitting areas originated in the United States and will certainly be copied abroad for its mixture of romanticism and practicality. Starting from the informal (if uncomfortable) custom of seating guests on cushions or on the floor at large parties, the 'conversation pit' is a solution that combines an intimate and impromptu atmosphere with the possibility of seating a lot of people without much furniture in a relatively small area. The room has a shallow well, whose walls can be used as seats or backrests. The examples shown here should give an idea of the various possibilities.

As the room grows in size, its arrangements change too. While bulky furniture – sofa, cabinet, and shelf units – are best placed against the wall in small rooms, they can now be placed free-standing in the room. Thus centers of gravity can be created. Whether the middle of the room is reserved for the sitting area or whether several zones of equal importance are formed by room dividers depends on personal taste and individual needs. Both possibilities are illustrated in Figs. 72-74.

The illustrations below show a loose arrangement articulated by light units, while on the opposite page the sitting area, with its compact, brightly colored furniture, governs the center of the room.

72

73

74

72, 73 This large, rectangular living room was made out of an old workshop by removing a partition. Movable shelf and storage units articulate the various functions of the room. The bookshelves and suspended cabinets serve as a room divider between the dining area and the living room (73); the slatted wooden mat, suspended from the ceiling, sets the tone for the restrained coloring of the sitting-room furniture and also serves to screen the storage space behind it. The natural-colored fiber carpet, with which the whole room is fitted, provides a neutral foil to the color scheme. The light furniture gives the room a casual and improvised air: a small desk with a telephone by the window, the easily shifted television set and the cupboard units on the two end walls, and finally transparent glass tops on metal frames for the coffee table and cocktail trolley.

74 This living room in a big new apartment has an obvious center and can be taken in at the first glance. In the middle a sitting area with strong color contrasts stands on a dark carpet in a strictly rectangular arrangement that matches the cube-like shapes of the upholstered furniture. The rear wall is completely taken up by a storage wall. On open shelves and in suspended cabinets books, radio, record player, television set, and a cocktail bar are housed. The diversity of open and closed compartments and the clear horizontal stress allow this wall to look lively and yet not overladen, despite its many storage facilities.

75

75   In this large and impressive living room in a detached house, it was possible to design the architectural features and the furniture to complement each other. Window walls running from floor to ceiling and interrupted only by a dark wooden storage wall determine the character of this light room. The floor of clear polished marble and the wooden ceiling in the same tones and with panels of corresponding size are well adapted to the restrained elegance of the room. The furniture too goes perfectly with these severe and definite outlines. Easy chairs on chromium-plated steel frames with leather upholstery were used for both sitting groups. In the background are six black Danish chairs on a light carpet, in the foreground natural-colored leather against the blue and green tones of the carpet. The room is illuminated by ceiling lamps with black shades and a row of built-in spotlights.

76

76   The massive fireplace built of rough-hewn red sandstone catches the
eye at once in this room. To contrast with its compact cubic shape a brightly
articulated storage unit was built into the recess toward the window. Open
shelves provide space for books, the television set, and collector's items.
Radio and record player are stored in low built-in cabinets, whose top
surface continues on below the large window in the end wall. In front of this
is the sitting area with its large couch in dark upholstery, supplemented by
two orange-colored easy chairs. In the foreground a bench placed against a
sideboard divides the room into living and dining areas. By moving the two
armchairs up, a second sitting group can be made around the open fire in the
evenings.

77

77, 78   In a family house in California with a beautiful view to the south, the living area was divided into two zones: a sitting area grouped about the fireplace and the end window wall, and a music center further back in the room where the glazed area is smaller. This features a grand piano and storage units for radio and record player. The recurring bays of the architectural grid can be recognized from within as the steel frame has been left exposed. The enclosed areas are wood, white plaster, or glass, and brown bricks have been used for the floor chimney. The proportions of the rectangular planes of diffe sizes and the interplay of the circular and triangular shape cylinder, cube, and sphere are carried through to the sma detail. Thus the over-all impression is very definite and rati and yet at the same time lively.

Two pale uncut-pile carpets clearly divide the room in two. sitting area in a strictly rectangular layout provides ca

81

On these pages four living rooms from three different countries are shown, all furnished in the strictly modern idiom. It would have been hard to guess which are from the United States (79, 82), which from Sweden (80), and which from Germany (81), because this style has been universally accepted across all frontiers. The clear arrangement of the furniture, with its contrast of severe cubes and organic shapes, is as typical as the interplay of contrasts in color and texture. Light metal frames for chairs and tables; cool marble and glass contrasted with soft carpets or shaggy rugs; a comfortable easy chair whose rounded shape is fitted to the contours of the body and whose vivid color introduces a lively note to the quiet background of the room; large curtain areas, plain or with discreet patterns, which add to the wall area rather than interrupt it; intimate lighting by standard lamps or low hanging lamps – these are a few of the principles applied in these rooms. Whether the problem is to find suitable furniture for a strictly modern setting (81, 82) or whether it is a case of refurbishing an old apartment (79, 80) this restrained, almost classical style is right for every occasion. These four examples show the range of possibilities within the same stylistic limitations.

83

84

83, 84 Low and lightweight furniture was chosen for this long attic room. The straightforward arrangement detracts from the feeling of confinement due to slanting walls. The entire room was painted white and fitted with a mottled black-and-gray fiber carpet. The short partition wall divides the room into two zones, a living-room area with a soft, natural-colored carpet and a light-covered settee, a table with a white plastic top, and two leather easy chairs (83); in the room beyond, two long wooden benches on a steel subframe with loose cushions turn the slanting wall into a sitting alcove. An American chaise-longue stands near the radio in charming contrast to the nineteenth-century Thonet rocking chair. The long sideboard with sliding doors provides ample storage space.

The attic room, once used for storage or as the maid's room, has recently acquired popularity. For the younger generation especially, its irregular shapes have all the appeal of the quaint and the romantic. While at one time slanting walls and visible beams were an obstacle which seemed to exclude rational furnishing, today they add to the special charm of these rooms. What may be lacking in window area and height, can be countered by a light color scheme and appropriate furnishings. Generally limited areas can be utilized without difficulty by modern low furniture.

85

86

85, 86 In the attic of an old house in Milan, with high windows and a rafter right across the room, a casual, apparently improvised arrangement of furniture seemed best. The disadvantages of the situation were overcome with a good deal of imagination. Two similar settees with covers in small checks were placed at angles, while a black easy chair and a low round table form a roomy and comfortable sitting corner. The continuous shelf below the window is meant for books and vases. The exposed rafter does not just serve merely as a support for the hanging lamp over the coffee table; it can display all sort of keepsakes. The unusually low picture is at the right height when seen from the sitting area. Here too, a nineteenth-century Thonet chair completes the furniture (86), whose unpretentious combination of old and new pieces results in an effective ensemble.

87

88

87, 88 Strong contrasts of modern and rustic styles come into play in the architecture and furniture of this large living room. Narrow wooden planks line the ceiling and long walls, while a parquet floor, brick wall, and enlarged map contribute textural variety. Light and shade have also been clearly distributed. The dark chimney corner is opposite a well-lit part of the room along the large window wall, in which the Le Corbusier chaise-longue, a painted peasant sideboard, and the grand piano constitute features but do not crowd the room. The two halves of the room are joined by the long bench with its dark upholstery.

89

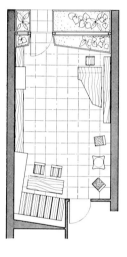

90

89, 90 In the living room of a small terraced house, the sitting corner was purposely moved away from the garden wall. An alcove-like recess is furnished by a bookshelf, the built-in cabinet for glasses and bottles, and a broad,comfortable couch (90) At right angles to this is a stone bench which provides more seats. A soft carpet stresses the intimate character of the corner, and large roof lights provide good even lighting. In contrast, the rest of the room with its polished stone floor was kept as free as possible (89). The rising wooden ceiling increases the volume of the room, while cabinet units and shelves on the long walls give the illusion of greater width. A flower bed let into the floor forms a link with the garden beyond. The modern harpsichord goes well with the shape of the room and the color of its woodwork.

91   To catch the sunlight even during the long winter months, this Swedish patio house has an inclined window wall. The installation of a short intermediate ceiling has interrupted the vertical direction of the large window without taking away much light; reflection from the whitewashed brick wall also serves to increase the illumination. The lively play of shadows, the climbing greenery of the plants, and the casual arrangement of the Scandinavian furniture create a homely atmosphere, which is stressed by the Swedish peasant carpets next to Persian rugs on the rough tiled floor.

91

92

92, 93   The elevated site of this detached house was a major influence in determining the position of the living room. The owner wished to command an undisturbed view of the magnificent city panorama while retaining an intimate atmosphere. That is why the fireplace corner was placed beside the large window. An alcove opening out to the front was created by the construction of a low false ceiling; the cozy character was stressed by fur rugs on the floor and window sill. The library was put further back in the room with a few chairs. The long, comparatively low plant window in the shelf wall (92) is an original idea.

93

94

95

94–99   Everyone agrees that the combination of new and old can not only create a harmonious ensemble but also set off each piece to great effect. How this is done, however, is as difficult as it is important. The choice of modern pieces must do justice to precious antique furniture and paintings. The photographs on these pages illustrate a large room in an Italian apartment whose furnishings have been assembled with faultless confidence. The dimensions of the rectangular room are almost those of a private gallery, an impression which is strengthened by the large white area of curtain on the window wall. A collection of antique furniture of different periods, valuable carpets, and old family portraits form the nucleus; the new purchases had to provide a place to sit near the fireplace, more seats near the radio, a desk for the owner, and a bookcase.

The room is divided into three parts but can be seen in its whole depth (98). If the curtain across the room behind the chimney sitting area (94) is pulled aside, the dining area (95) behind it is visible. This reveals the charming effect of a *trompe l'oeil* because the two identical sideboards separated by the

96

curtain seem to be a mirror image of each other (97). In the other direction
a free-standing modern shelf unit with built-in record player divides off the
sitting area around the radio without hiding it completely. Next to this,
toward the window, stands the desk, a glass-topped table with suspended
drawer unit, and a seventeenth-century armchair.

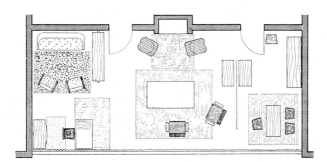

97

98

99

A table similar to the desk but lower serves as a coffee table before the fireplace (94). Four modern easy chairs complete this group. The curvilinear shape of the cane chairs, light the in weight and coloring, contrasts with the green upholstery of the wing chairs. Bulky furniture was consciously avoided in order to set off the sideboards, pictures, and carpets to the best advantage.

Each individual group is confined and enhanced by carpets. The large paintings are reserved for the living area. The charm of these family portraits has been stressed by simple frames and unconventional but not contrived hanging (99). It was a particularly clever, typically Italian idea to attach the portrait of a lady in the dining area to a pole so that it can be turned to one side or the other. The whole room is lit solely by adjustable ceiling spots, so that no lamps disturb this already rich ensemble.

100

101

100, 101   Similar problems arose during the furnishing of this large room in the apartment of a New York art collector. Here, as in the previous example, two living areas and a dining area were to be combined with a collection of important works of art. The plan made a logical division easier: the dining room to the rear (100) can be shut off by a sliding door, as can the library with its television set and radio (101). The most striking aspect of this room is the imaginative combination of old and modern in both art and furniture (100).

103

104

102–104 This large living room furnished for himself by an architect in an old house in San Francisco Bay (see also 56, 166, 260, 317, 318) shows the self-confidence which united aesthetic and practical considerations in a harmonious whole, despite the diversity of elements. Patches of light and shade alternate with one another, wall areas are divided up, groups formed, and the smallest details considered with love and care. The owner's passion for collecting is obvious from the furniture. It is composed of very different pieces: old sea chests and folk pieces, and nineteenth-century bentwood chairs next to modern upholstered furniture. The unpretentious, meaningful arrangement avoids a contrived or staged flavor. Light curtains and the timber-paneled chimney wall give the sitting area warmth, which is further enhanced by the large white fur rug (104, 56). The subdivided bookcase wall with illuminated compartments for works of art leads into the open part of the room. The adjoining plant window faces a staircase and a work area with a large desk shelf (103).

THE FIREPLACE

'The installation of an open fireplace in human habitations marks the beginning of all domestic culture' – this is what one reads in a treatise on the historical development of the hearth. Considering the progress of civilization, it is somewhat surprising that we are still sitting round the 'open fire' in this age of central heating and air-conditioning.

Apart from all questions of mere use, the fascinating play of the firelight has enchanted people since time immemorial. And it is this enchantment above all which keeps us gathered round the fire today. Unconditional following of fashion and a tendency toward mistaken grandeur must be avoided in present times. The decorative character of a fireplace should be considered just as much as the financial and architectural problems which its installation entails. Once the decision has been made, there is a multitude of possibilities, which range from the built-in fireplace (138) in a small apartment that looks like part of the furniture, to the large fireplace in a detached house (76) which dominates the room. One principle should always be remembered: a fireplace that is not suitable for the center of a sitting area – even if only by moving chairs and stools around it – is as illogical to day as a bookcase without books. When you look through the following pages, do not be misled into thinking that this requirement has occasionally been disregarded, as the sitting-room furniture often has been pushed aside when the photograph was taken in order to bring out certain details. On the other hand, examples prove what a wide range there really is in the architectural forms of fireplace design. The traditional type of fireplace, with its position in the exact center of the wall, its obligatory mantelpiece, and sometimes a mirrored overmantel, has undoubted historical charm but is not always in keeping with the modern style of living. Modern architecture has fundamentally altered this: symmetrical arrangement and framed surrounds are avoided so that only the graphic effect of the hole in the wall (109) or the interplay of materials and shapes (110, 113) is important. Less conventional solutions include types which articulate the room with free-standing models; occasionally these serve to divide the room up into zones (116–119). Finally, the fireplace can even become a sculptural, artistic shape (120).

105

105 The massive strength of rough-hewn stone, with projecting shelves and a window-like void produce an effect of great power in this living room. Fireplaces in many cases are no longer merely chosen by the criterion of usefulness. The conclusion was drawn here that it could become a free shape of artistic value.

106

country house (105), the fireplace was unobtrusively incorporated into this Swedish
room; the brick lining is continued below
the stairs and the color of the chimney piece
is the same as that of the wall plaster.

107

107   When an old Danish farmhouse was rebuilt, the fireplace was left just as it had been for hundreds of years. In the center of the room stands the massive fireplace of whitewashed bricks, which continues upward through the house as a chimney. The huge fireplace opens into the former kitchen over a high base for easy cleaning. The surrounding rooms are also heated by radiation.

108   This traditional Scandinavian fireplace was installed in a house in Copenhagen. The simple rectilinear shapes go well with the rustic character of the large room. By placing the chimney stack in the outside wall, it was possible to build an outdoor barbecue whose flue enters the same chimney.

108

109

110

109, 110 The fireplaces in these two small Danish houses are situated on the narrow wall of the long living room. The fireplace walls and the room are sufficiently empty to reveal the contours and shapes to full advantage. In the upper picture the fireplace consists of a rectangular slit in the whitewashed wall; in the lower one, it is built up of blocks, and the whitewashed rectangle appears to float in space. In the evening, easy chairs, hassocks, and cushions can be grouped round the fire.

111

112

111   The large brick fireplace wall is the center of gravity in this Swiss living room. The fire opening and recess for logs have been placed side by side below a narrow dark marble mantelpiece. The hearth, which is usually essential, could be eliminated here because a continuous marble slab projects forward to catch the sparks.

112   The same way of storing logs has been used in this American house. The white-washed fireplace wall is richly subdivided by niches and compartments and can thus provide the backdrop for new decorative effects. The silhouette-like tracery of the fire irons is particularly charming.

To save the master of the house constant journeys to the woodpile, the problem arises of how to store huge logs in the immediate vicinity of the fireplaces. When baskets and troughs are not sufficient a built-in recess next to the fireplace provides a decorative and practical solution. The two pictures on the opposite page (111, 112) illustrate how the shapes and textures of stacked logs contribute to the décor of the room.

It was not until the advent of modern architecture, with its tendency to the open plan, that free-standing fireplaces came into general use. The examples shown here (113–121) are all from America and Scandinavia, where this practice has been most fully developed. While in other countries a room divider or partition might have been inserted between floor and ceiling, the architects here have boldly situated the chimney in the center of the room. It serves as a room divider with a massive architectonic effect. The free-standing fireplace has numerous practical advantages. For example, the back wall can, if properly insulated, provide storage space for books (113,115). Elsewhere the chimney can be left open on both sides to warm each half of the room (114). In the three examples on this page the fireplace is used to separate living room from library. This arrangement provides the right atmosphere for both entertaining and quiet reading.

113

114

115

113   White plastered fireplace wall with black sheet-metal canopy. Fire immediately above the stone floor on wrought-iron trivet.

114   Double fireplace with white plaster wall. The brick lining of the fireplace is carried through to the outside as a narrow frame.

115   The fireplace base is a large block of natural stone. The left-hand wall is of exposed brick; the right-hand one is plastered. The canopy is made of black sheet metal.

116

The fireplaces in two large American living rooms show particularly well what new and surprising results can be achieved in interior decoration by the use of unconventional materials. Traditional materials can be used, as well as those which are usually associated with exteriors, like concrete. In Fig. 116 the fireplace wall and rear wall of the room were constructed of rough-hewn stone and then white-washed, a procedure known since the early days of building. The combination of a glass side wall, tiled floor, and wooden ceiling, gives a well-balanced composition despite all the contrasts, and the restrained, simple lines of the furniture match it well. The upper part of the fireplace wall finishes in a continuous window strip, so that the wall appears less massive, and its delicate relief is shown to better effect.

The large rooms in Figs. 120, 121 are fully glazed toward the lake and are separated into dining and living room by the huge fireplace. The concrete fireplace unit looks like a piece of sculpture and has been treated as such. The surface has been boasted with a chisel to give a coarse-grained surface. Big sharp-edged apertures have been cut into the wall to afford views into the areas beyond. The softly modeled shape of the white chimney forms a contrast with the rectilinear block. This splendid large-scale conception is carried through to every detail of the furnishings.

117

118

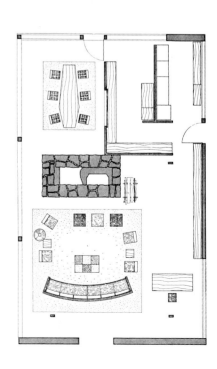

119

Two open-plan rooms in American houses illustrate other chimney-wall possibilities. Above (119), a large, long room with two functional zones is divided by the chimney wall, which projects at right angles from the side wall as far as the center of the room. The partition was built of whitewashed hollow blocks; above the fireplace, which is open at both sides, it consists of rough-hewn natural stone. A cantilevered bench faced with dark tiles serves as a low table surface and catches the sparks so that the wall-to-wall carpet can be carried up right to the base of the fireplace. In the foreground is the spacious sitting area, in the room beyond, the library with more seats, and in the far background, a breakfast bar with view into the kitchen.

120, 121   Entrance, living-dining area, and kitchen are all grouped together in one big rectangular room. The long fireplace wall separates the entrance hall from the living-room corner but extends only to shoulder height, so that both rooms are connected above it. The masonry of the fireplace and its cylindrical chimney, as well as the walls of the hall and kitchen, have a white plaster surface, while dark wood was used for the rear wall of the living room, the cabinet in the hall, and the furniture. Thus there is an interplay of contrasts between light and dark surfaces from the various viewpoints.

120

121

RADIO AND TELEVISION SETS

We may welcome or condemn it: television has become an integral part of daily life. In America and the larger European countries television viewers may be counted in millions and the number of new viewers is constantly growing. A radio can be placed anywhere, whereas a television set alters the room. It makes demands which must be considered if reception is not to suffer considerably. Often, a regrouping of the furniture or a change of lighting is essential. A television set always introduces an element of the technical into a room, which may be either stressed or neutralized but must in any case be taken into consideration. A minimum distance between seats and screen is essential. Viewed from too close, the television image dissolves into the horizontal parallel lines from which it is made up; only at a certain distance do the disruptive lines disappear. This minimum distance is calculated by the height of the screen multiplied by five. Thus it amounts to approximately 6'7" for a screen image 19" × 15" (screen width 21" or 23"). The viewing angle at which the image is free of distortion is approximately 60° from the center of the screen and the arrangement of the chairs should take account of this. As a bright television screen in a dark room can tire the eyes, a light wall area next to or behind the set will counteract eyestrain. This surrounding wall illumination can be achieved by a special light fixed to the back of the set. The solutions illustrated on the following pages are divided into two main groups: those in which the television or radio set is incorporated in imaginative unit furniture or wall alcoves (125, 127–134, 137–140), and those where it is openly displayed (122, 124, 126). The choice depends upon aesthetic factors as much as it does upon the frequency with which the set is used. In each case one must decide whether the empty glass screen strikes a disturbing note or whether it can contribute to the over-all design of the room.

122

122 Compared to sets which are built into storage walls or shelves, free-standing sets have the advantage of greater flexibility. This set combining radio and television is movable on casters; in addition, the screen can be turned around and swiveled. The set can therefore serve different sitting areas and does not immobilize the furniture, as is often the case with built-in television sets.

123

123   Modern unit furniture is often well adapted to house a television set. By leaving out one shelf in this Swedish red lacquered cabinet-bookcase, enough room has been created for a standard table model. Placing a set in a shelf unit creates two problems, however. First, the set gives off a considerable amount of heat and needs ventilation, and second, table models with their loudspeakers at the side may have these blocked by uprights so that sound production suffers. New pieces of furniture have been specially devised by the manufacturers for television viewers, as for instance the 'television couch' or the easy chair with matching stool, which can be seen above.

124

The television set determines how furniture shall be placed within a room. The French example (124) is distinguished by its flexibility. Located between two parts of the living room, the set can be rotated to face the sitting area, which contains light, easily movable chairs. In the other two examples (125, 126) the viewing angle has determined the placing of the furniture, which either faces or stands at right angles to the set. The screen should be situated at a height corresponding with that of the viewer's eyes, usually about 2′ 8″ to 3′ 3″ from the floor to the center of the screen.

124   The technical installations in this sitting area have been very charmingly devised. A group of two shell seats and a bench seat, to which the square easy chairs from the living room in the background can be added, is related to the television set placed on a wall bracket. The screen is situated with its back to the window, so that daylight, which can be excluded by Venetian blinds, does not interfere with daytime reception. The loudspeaker is another decorative feature: its mustard-yellow material stands out against the whitewashed brick wall and its rectangular shape is set off by a pattern of leaves and tendrils. Both aesthetic and practical considerations have come into equal play in this cultivated but by no means contrived room arrangement.

125

126

125 Built-in unit with bookshelves and suspended cabinets in front of a veneered wall. One cabinet contains the television set, the other a cocktail bar; each can be closed off by folding doors. The severity of the horizontally arranged cabinet units corresponds with the rectangular arrangement of the heavy square couch and chairs.

126 This built-in divan table provides a particularly light and elegant base for the television set. Naturally, however, its situation precludes the use of the divan a sa seat for watching the set.

127

It is not always in accordance with the style of a room or the wishes of its occupants for a television set to be openly displayed. An American art collector wished to avoid the discordant contrast that an array of technical equipment would make with his collection of objets d'art (127, 128). The cupboard and shelf wall shown in Figs. 129 and 130 is so effective in itself with its white framed divisions and open and closed compartments that it was thought best to conceal the television set when it was not in use.

128

127, 128 The wall recess houses not only the television set on a retractable shelf but also – at a less accessible height – the radio, phonograph, and record rack. All these pieces of equipment are hidden behind a decorated sliding door, a device which recalls the secret doors in old castles. Below the television set, a loudspeaker was built into the flat projection, which also serves as a bench.

129, 130 Built-in storage wall with cabinets, bookshelves, and high cupboards that also continue over the door (129 right). The television set is in a cabinet that projects beyond the others on account of the depth of the set. Radio and record player are behind a hinged lattice grille. The concealed lighting above the bookshelves is useful when the equipment is being used.

130

129

131, 132 Furniture specially designed for the apartment of a young New York actress (see also 489–494). The unit comprises a writing desk by the window, a record cabinet, a record player in a drawer, a radio behind a sliding door, and a swivel device for the television set. The set, which has a cabinet of its own, is portable.

132

131

133

134

133, 134   The various pieces of equipment, including a tape-recorder, have all been combined in a wall of sound equipment, where every unit is within easy reach: television set at the right height for seated viewers, tape-recorder at an inclined angle, the radio with the tuning dial easily visible. The remaining compartments accommodate record albums and books. Below the ceiling is a built-in loudspeaker. The 'wall of sound' and the cocktail bar next to it can be closed off by sliding doors, which have been related in width to the distances between the ceiling beams. The flexibility of the furniture and the general lightness of effect in this American example recall the Japanese manner.

135

136

135, 136 The imaginative combination of cabinets and fireplace in this Milan apartment creates a dividing wall between living and dining rooms. At lower left the cabinets contain radio, phonograph, and records; above runs a row of additional cabinets with laminated-plastic sliding doors that can be opened from both rooms. On top a glass panel separates the rooms up to the ceiling. The view from the dining room (136) shows the back of the music cabinet and a series of drawers in graded depths on the right. The room's essential simplicity has been enlivened by strong colors: yellow ceiling, red floor tiles, walnut woodwork, dark-brown enameled chimney canopy, and dark-brown couch. The white fronts of the radio and loudspeaker and the graphic pattern of knobs and loudspeaker grille are of outstanding decorative value.

137

137 A shallow wall recess was utilized for an original combination of shelf and alcove in this Italian example, an improvised construction of light appearance which provides much additional space. The record player and radio let into the wall can be closed off by a sliding door. The fittings are entirely of teak, with the exception of birchwood partitions in the record rack.

138, 139 In this example an L-shaped furniture unit encloses the sitting corner in the living room of a fairly old French house. The items featured include a bench seat with removable upholstery, a brick-lined open fireplace, and built-in cabinets. The unit on the left of the fire, which is easily reached from the seat, houses the records and the record player. All the component elements are topped by one continuous shelf, which is transformed into a bookcase at the left by the addition of a few extra shelves.

138

139

140

141

140, 141 This cabinet wall covered with walnut veneer separates the entrance hall from the living room. It houses the radio and phonograph, and also a film projector that is controlled from the other side of the partition. A white plastic door conceals the projector and record player; tuning dials are lodged in the two panels immediately below. Records are stored in the upper cabinets. At the side, a bookcase with a telephone shelf has been built into the cabinet wall.

142

142 In contrast to the entirely closed surface of Figs. 140 and 141, this cabinet wall has been articulated by the alternation of open and closed spaces. Desk, cocktail bar, and radio are all built-in.

BOOKCASE AND DESK

The nineteenth century loved the heavy glazed bookcase. Nowadays, however, since book bindings and protective covers have become more attractive and durable, open shelves are used everywhere. It is more important for books to be easily accessible than to be remote objects on display. Only owners of rare books or antique bookcases keep their books behind panels of glass or wood today. The amount of space needed for books varies constantly in this age of pocket editions and paperbacks. Built-in and unit bookcases with adjustable shelf heights and easily added parts are just the thing to house a constantly growing collection.

143

143, 144 The modern taste for furniture of light appearance extends to bookcases as well as to movable furnishings. These Italian bookshelves are supported by brackets hooked into slotted metal strips. The white enameled shelves stand out against the dark background, giving the impression of floating construction. The distance between shelves can be easily adjusted according to the height of the books. Other items, such as the writing surface with a light above it, can be incorporated into the bookcase without difficulty.
Shelves on metal supports have been fitted in front of the window, which opens only at the top. The tapering of the shelves enhances the general effect of lightness. Diffuse light from the window, silhouetting any objects placed against it, makes these window ledges ideal for the display of collector's pieces.

145

These two storage walls (145, 146) have a very different effect. In Fig. 145 the bookcase, low furniture, open fireplace, and the sloping, boarded ceiling form an intimate ensemble. The bookcase on the right-hand page (146), supported by black enameled rods, gives an impression of imposing severity. The shelves are evenly spaced in order that their continuous lines may stress a horizontal axis. The rectangular arrangement of the furniture is in keeping with the simple but bold features of the bookcase.

145   The bookcase is made of solid vertical members, which support unmovable built-in shelves; this gives the impression of a series of rectangular boxes. On the right, the height of each shelf was kept low; 8½ to 9 inches is usually sufficient for most books. The shape of the room, the sloping ceiling, and the window opening were cleverly taken into account. The deep-set window casing has been filled with plants, so that one scarcely notices the radiator below.

146

146   Mat black enameled tubular-steel frame, with shelves and cupboard
units in teak. The unit was designed to fit the measurements of the room.
By omitting two shelves, a telephone recess, illuminated by a strip light, was
made. The chair in front of the recess differs from those around the dining
table by having a blue seat instead of a white one.

147   Wall cupboard, radiator cage, and bookshelves grouped to form one unit. The shelves are not adjustable. The top one has circular cut-outs to hold plants.

148   In this example a shelf unit takes up the whole of one narrow wall of a living room study. The frame, constructed of square bars, is strengthened not only by the lower horizontal cupboard units which house radio and record player, but also by additional metal bars below the shelves. The whitewashed wall behind the structure reflects concealed lighting and thus emphasizes the transparent effect of the graceful unit. The tubular light above the desk is covered by a metal shade.

147

148

149

The shelves of these bookcases rest on brackets clipped into the uprights. This system, with its freely supported bookshelves, is elegant but demands firm anchoring of the metal units for the structure to support the weight of the books.

149   The many variations permitted by the use of slotted strips and brackets can be increased by varying the width and depth of the shelves. In this ensemble, with its apparently casual disposition of shelves and unconventionally arranged objets d'art, the decorative over-all effect was as important as the housing of the library.

150   Slotted metal bookcase with shelves of varying depths and heights, and a suspended cabinet. Independent lighting of book wall by tubular lights.

150

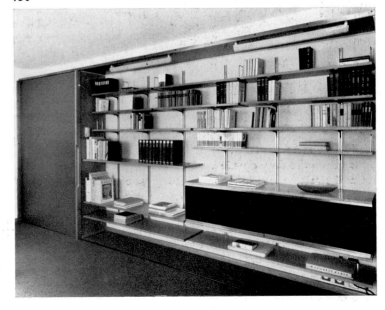

151

152

Bookcases can be adapted to the most widely varying room conditions. In both these examples (151, 152) the shelves continue above the door opening. In the slotted-rail example (151) it was desirable to continue the unified effect of the horizontally divided wall and to neutralize the strong pattern of paneling, coffered door, and cornice by slender bookshelves. The lowest compartment thus provides an attractive toy-shelf for a younger child. In addition, both examples are save space, as can be seen from the Swedish bookcase made of solid elm. Here, too, the shelves are adjustable. Alcoves below windows or unused doors provide further opportunities for building in shelves.

153

154

Thanks to their visual weightlessness and unob-
trusiveness, modern bookcases can serve to display
works of art and similar objects without distracting
the beholder.

In the apartment of an Italian art collector (153),
suspended shelves and wall cabinets are related in
their lightweight effect to the casual arrangement
of the pictures on the right and the Rococo armchair placed on a projecting shelf of glass. Individually hung shelves can of course support only a
limited weight. The example on the right (154)
contrasts the ordered symmetry of metal rails and
bookshelves with the comfortable shape of the
Baroque armchair.

155

156

155, 156 A wall recess was cleverly utilized for this unit of bookcase, cabinets, desk, and drawers. By aligning the component parts vertically, the designer has balanced the horizontal direction of the framed bookcase. The lower cabinets project and the shelf top thereby created continues the mantelpiece above the brick fireplace at the right. The bookcase has sliding glass doors and glass shelves.

In most houses that have no separate library, books are generally kept in the living room. But books are also needed in other rooms. A small shelf in the kitchen for cookbooks, a shelf in the nursery (429), a shelf in the bedroom (347), and above all a few shelves near the writing table (157–167) always prove useful. Here we keep the books we need for reference: dictionaries, encyclopedias, and manuals.

157   A few shelves and a cupboard whose hinged front is a writing surface when open have been fitted between two timber uprights. Desk and shelves have been inserted into the slotted fittings on clips; the uprights are screwed to floor and ceiling. An adjustable wall light also serves the desk.

157

158

158   In this apartment in an old house the chimney creates an area of dead space which seems to defy any possible furnishing. A writing table, however, can still be fitted there, especially as daylight enters from the left. The beveled writing surface with a timber dado behind it makes clever use of available space. Glass was used for the shelves of the small bookcase to counteract any sense of overcrowding. The space below the windowsill also takes a bookcase.

159

The writing table in a living room should be spatially isolated. This is easily done where the shape of a room permits it to be divided into functional zones. But even in a small rectangular room the separation of the desk can be achieved by an ingenious arrangement of the furniture. This is illustrated by the Swedish living room (159), in which the leather easy chairs of the sitting area are placed with their backs to the desk. The bookcase, too, usually an integral part of the writing corner, can take over the function of separating and setting apart when it is used as a room divider (160).

160

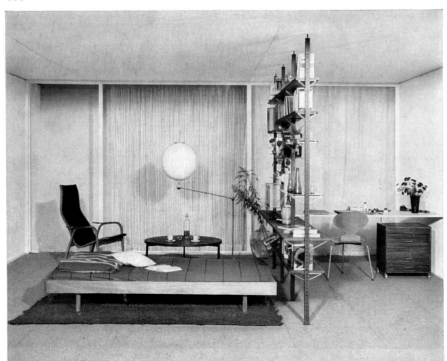

161

159   A living room which has been divided up by simple means. The two centers –
sitting area and well-lit writing table – are each outlined by rugs. Each area has its
own focus: the sitting area looks toward the fireplace, the desk to the opposite
wall. The uprights of the bookcase serve as bookends and are provided with hooks
to support the shelves.

160   Sitting room and desk have been visually separated by a bookcase placed at
right angles to the room. The shelves are supported by brackets fixed to the
uprights. A particularly broad shelf meets the writing surface at right angles.
Below the writing surface stands a teak chest of drawers on casters.

161   The large size and irregular plan of this American living room made it
possible to separate the working area, which is furnished with an armchair, a desk
on square steel legs, and hanging bookshelves. The shelves are widely spaced so
as not to interfere with the decorative effect of the wood paneling.
The elegant color scheme of the room is restricted to light brown, light gray, and
white and unites both areas. Similarly, the wood paneling continues into the living
room. The magnificent old swivel chair and the soft carpet ensure that the room
is not too austere.

162

163

165

164

162–164 In this French apartment the desk is accommodated in an anteroom that opens into the living room but is differentiated from it by a low ceiling of wooden boards. Like the long, narrow shelf unit above, the writing surface is supported at one end by the wall and at the other by the pillar, which it partially encloses. The varying depth of the desk surface thus creates an alcove to hold books needed while working. The area is lit by a strip light covered with frosted glass. This solution, with its emphasis on simplicity, is decorative as well as functional.

165 A smaller desk with writing surface and a suspended drawer. An adjustable wall lamp provides illumination.

In a detached house or duplex apartment, the space in front of or below the staircase is nearly always wasted. It can be transformed by the simplest means into a writing corner, a work area for children, or a telephone nook. Unfortunately there is rarely enough daylight in these corners and one must supplement it with lamps.

166

167

166   A cantilevered writing surface, two bentwood chairs, and two hanging lamps make writing space for two in an American house. The drawer below the writing surface is kept shallow so that it does not take up leg room. The shelves on the right contain a card index and other small items.

167   A writing surface on a white-enameled cupboard; below the stairs a small shelf has been fixed. The pegboard on the rear wall is sound-absorbant. This place is not intended for work taking any length of time but only for a few short notes during a telephone conversation.

THE PLANT WINDOW

Plants in the home make much the same direct appeal to the emotions as does an open fire. Cut flowers, potted plants, or a roof garden help bring nature back into the everyday existence of people who live in cities of cement and steel. In the nineteenth century attempts were made to bring nature back into the home by means of the winter garden, or conservatory. The winter garden was a separate room, a sort of small greenhouse, which substituted for the garden inaccessible in winter. The plant window, which has taken its place today, tries to bring a piece of nature into the house all the year round. It is not surprising that a number of excellent examples come from Scandinavia where the summers are short.

The simplest form of plant window involves a few plant pots on a broad flower board, which has been covered with some impervious material (ceramic, stone, or plastic). A sunken or boarded trough, watertight and filled with pebbles, can be used to conceal the pots. The plants are set into the soil in pans which contain a layer of humus over pebbles; drainage is essential to eliminate root rot. Very expensive plant windows have glass on both sides (172). In this way ideal climatic conditions can be created. No longer exposed to dry central heating, the plants retain moisture and do not need constant watering. Besides this, the inner pane provides heat insulation for the living room. On the other hand, the all-enclosed plant window has the disadvantage of being visually separated from the room.

Plants and flowers are no hobby for lazy people; an understanding of the rhythm of their growth and flowering is essential. They are not objects for exhibition but living organisms which demand attention. When plants are subjected to south light, some form of protection is nearly always necessary: awnings, metal blinds, or plastic or wooden slats. These sun shades are best fixed in front of windows, to increase reflection. Few indoor plants can tolerate drafts. Their need for water varies, so that different plants in the same trough have to be carefully grouped. Finally, not just common sense, but luck too, is necessary for indoor plants to flourish.

168 The floor bed has the advantage of letting plants appear not only as silhouettes against the window opening but also as a green carpet when viewed from above. In this Danish house, ivy and vines twine round the window and form a link with the vegetation outside. The clever use of irregularly jointed flagstones contributes to an extraordinarily lively asymmetrical arrangement. The left side of the window is stressed, a feature which is underlined by the placing of the lamp. A venetian blind affords protection from the sun; it should be fixed in front of the window to increase reflection.

169

Plant windows can be related to interiors and exteriors in the most diverse manner. In the Swedish example (169) the plants do not extend beyond the window frame, but their varied shapes make a pleasant balance for the severe and imposing lines of the furniture, the leather-upholstered easy chairs, and the square glass-topped table. The lower plant window (170), with gnarled tree trunk, contrasts with both the shape of the window and the tall slender trees in the garden. In the German example (171), the shrubs in the garden are echoed by the plants in the window. The narrow strip of lawn seems to lead right into the room, with the window as an open gate into nature.

169   The potted plants have been grouped almost casually in an arrangement that is flexible yet does justice to each plant. The pebble-filled trough provides drainage. When the plants have luxuriant foliage, one can even dispense with curtains.

170

170   The gnarled, decomposing trunk sets the theme; on it the leafy plants look like tropical parasites. The vegetation takes up much of the window area and is intended to produce a silhouette effect; Japanese examples have obviously been the inspiration here. The frame of the plant window was lined with natural stone to provide the rustic frame for a fantastic and exotic piece of nature.

171

171 For the planting of this window a selection was made of almost exclusively native plants, and these form a harmonious ensemble with the
vegetation in the garden. The high-climbing tendrils surround the right-
hand side of the square window and prepare one for the organic shapes of
the world outside. An awning offers protection from the sun. The plant
trough is edged with tiles that match the floor. To shut off the living room
from the outside world, a curtain can be drawn in front of the plant window,

172

173

172 Plant windows running the entire width of the wall determine the character of a room. The arrangement of this dining room complements the plants' lively silhouettes by using furniture of simple design and by leaving a free space in front of the window. The plant window is glazed toward the room by a sliding frameless pane, and this creates a particularly favorable atmosphere for the plants. The impression of a showcase, which the glazed plant window evokes, has been consciously stressed. In the ceiling above the trough is a recessed light covered by a glass screen. The strong contrasts of the plants – from stiff cacti and gnarled branches to climbing plants – are emphasized by the interplay of light and shade. White plastic Venetian blinds afford protection from the sun.

174

175

173 The thickly planted window, a bookcase with shelves of very light-weight appearance, an antique table, and a chair make up a pleasant writing corner. The window contains vines, a small tree, and plants which cascade downward from hanging baskets. Here, as with any imaginative device in interior decoration, one must take care to avoid the trick effect of temporary and ostentatious fads.

174 A ground-level bed where the vegetation forms a delightful contrast to the rectangular lines of the floor slabs and the shape of the bed itself. It consists of a trough sunk into the floor, providing a visual continuation of the plants growing outside. The tropical plants on the inside repeat the contours of native plants in the garden. Here, as in all the other examples, the depth of the plant window or indoor bed is no more than 32 inches; this depth should not be exceeded if the plants are to be looked after easily.

175 Where architectural conditions do not permit built-in sunken troughs, box containers can be placed in front of the window. The bamboo side wall serves as a trellis for climbing plants.

The combined living-dining room

The combined living-dining room

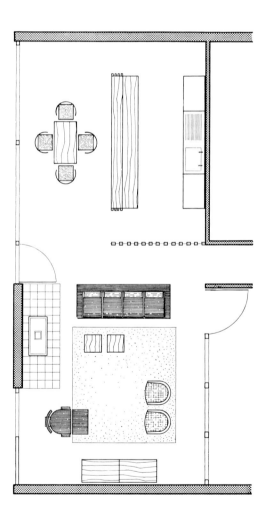

176 (page 120) Open layout in an American house with living area and fireplace, dining area and kitchen as functional zones in a large continuous room. The living area is separated from the rest of the room by placing the couch with its back to the dining area and kitchen.

Such rooms as that on page 120 (176) were thought extreme as recently as thirty years ago and only readers of avant-garde architectural magazines would have been sympathetic to them. Today we are all so familiar with the type of development exemplified here that we see in this solution an acceptable possibility, if not the ideal answer to the problem.

What does this example show us? It is proof of our changing conceptions of space. No longer do we live in separate cells whose monotonous box shape is at most interrupted by an alcove or projection. Many people today equate modern style with the disappearance or at least partial suspension of room limits for the sake of spaciousness. Whereas our grandparents kept symmetry as their guiding principle, we enjoy the charm of the surprise view and changing vistas. The open plan is an ideal of our times.

Behind all this is first and foremost an aesthetic maxim. On its account we even put up with such disadvantages as the unavoidable noises and cooking smells of a combined living-dining room. Even social changes and simple practical reasons play a part.

Let us look at our example: in the background on the left, in front of the room-high window, is an alcove furnished as a dining area opening out of the main room. On the right is the kitchen, visually separated by a wooden grille with a large hatch into the dining area. Spaciousness and an almost unrestricted view are the principal features. Beyond the formal aspect there is a practical advantage: kitchen and dining room are only a few steps apart;

dishes and food are simply put down on the hatch table, which also serves as a counter. This saves a lot of work, as unnecessary steps and manipulations are avoided, and is of particular importance where a housewife has to do her own chores without outside help, a common enough situation in this age of labor shortage. Furthermore, statistics have proved that the housewife spends four to six hours a day in the kitchen. Why should she be completely cut off from the family during this time? On the principle that life within the community should first be tried out in the family circle as the smallest social unit, why not involve the members of the family to a certain degree in the work of the household? To the extent that this depends on considerations of space, the open plan is ideal. One last point: although children are a nuisance in the kitchen, the mother usually wants to keep them under supervision. If they play in the living or dining area and can be watched from the kitchen, this is no longer any problem.

As regards furniture, too, our example is most instructive. It makes it clear that the open plan imposes certain conditions on furnishing. Tall or bulky furniture would destroy the newly won spaciousness. That is why light, adaptable, and sparsely distributed furniture with low individual pieces should be chosen for such a room. The few existing wall areas should not be hidden but incorporated as a frame to set off the whole ensemble. Cupboards are built into the walls, unless one desires to give the room a highlight by featuring some particularly beautiful antique piece. Textures can create the atmosphere of a room in this by means of graining of the light wooden ceiling, the dark stained beams, and the warm tone of the cork floor. The assumption that all this can be achieved only after considerable expense is contradicted by our example, which an architect built for his own family to prove that this solution is actually cheaper to build than the ordinary kind of house.

How can the open- plan principle be applied to an apartment in a block of flats? One large room which combines different functions, at least those of living and eating, makes this possible. Architects comply more and more with this desire for spaciousness in new buildings by designing generously proportioned main rooms and by adding the area of the former dining room to that of the living room. Hence, as a rule, we get a long rectangular room with windows on the long wall. The furnishing is usually left to individual choice unless a hatch determines the position of the dining table.

177

177 This dining area in a long room is differentiated from the living area by the dark rug underneath the table and chairs. The door to the kitchen is at the back of the room. A third zone, with fireplace, rug, and bookshelves, is visible in the background.

178 Zones created by vertical room-dividers in a living-dining room: on the right a screen of natural wood fabric, on the left a free-standing storage unit which serves to enclose the living area. Behind it is the dining area.

178

Where this is not the case, the sitting area can be located by the window or against the back wall; the dining table can be placed next to a wall or else stand freely in the room. The only criterion is the diversity of function which requires that dining and living areas should be more or less strongly differentiated. Zones can be marked off in a number of different ways. One of the most popular is shown in Fig. 177: the dining area is on the right against the long wall; the sitting area in the left foreground. Both zones are accentuated by dark rugs, while the rest of the room is fitted with a light-colored velour carpet. The arrangement of furniture can also divide areas up as in Fig. 176 where the couch has been placed with its back to the dining area. Low bookcases, sideboards, or chests can serve the same purpose. The subdivision becomes even more definite when temporary walls such as curtains or sliding partitions are employed. Sometimes it is even possible to replace a solid wall in this way and thus eliminate most smells and noises from the kitchen. An intermediate solution is the room-divider of shelves or cabinets, which separates areas visually without altogether closing them off. Finally, subdivision can be effected by architectural elements. These must be planned when the house or apartment is designed, for it is difficult and expensive to install them later.

To this category of room-dividers belong free-standing fireplaces, balustrades, and different levels. A more important and more frequently employed device is the addition of an alcove or the building-on of a wing to produce an L-shape. In these cases, the largest part of the room is reserved for the living area while the smaller one is for dining. With this we are back at the prototype (176) with which we started. Further examples of the open plan with consecutive room areas follow at the end of the chapter.

179

The given situation of the rooms on the following four pages is the same in each case: a rectangular room of the dimensions usual in a medium-sized apartment. They have neither alcoves nor serving hatches, so only the practical consideration of distance between kitchen and table determined the placing of the dining areas. One can see that there is no standard way of arranging such a room. A frequent practice is to put the sitting area far back in the room (183), but there are just as many examples where the living area is near the window (182). Two significant principles emerge for the relationship of sitting and dining areas. In one case both zones are exactly defined, as though an invisible wall cut the room into two independent parts (180, 181). In the other case, the zones intermingle. In Fig. 179, for example, the storage wall unites both halves of the room. The furniture is arranged in a flexible plan, and because the two focal areas lie in opposite corners of the room, one feels no conflict between parts.

179   The dominant feature of this room is the long storage wall. The casual arrangement of the books and objects on the shelves imparts an agreeable air of improvisation to the room. The dining and writing areas are near the window and consist of two tables pushed together to form an L-shape. In the foreground is the sitting area, and opposite it on the shelf stand the television set and radio.

180, 181   A strictly geometrical room with the living area arranged like a separate room; its furniture is placed round the periphery, leaving the center free. An armchair and a table on casters shut it off from the dining area. Suspended shelves on each end wall mirror each other.

180

181

182

183

182   Two sofa-beds define the living area by their L-shaped arrangement. The square dining table is sufficiently far away from the wall to allow four people to sit comfortably around it. Carpets of the same color emphasize the two zones, which are arranged one behind the other along the left-hand wall. In the right-hand half of the room, a continuous strip remains free. Apart from standard and wall lamps there is a third source of light, a lamp at the left with an adjustable arm that can be swiveled around to serve the dining table or the sitting area.

184

185

183   A room whose furniture, wallpaper, and textiles have a Biedermeier character. The sitting area and oval dining table are arranged diagonally across the room. The living area is at the back while the center of the room remains empty. Two carpet runners of different widths make the room look longer and tie the two areas together. The wing chair and the cabinet also serve to unite the room rather than divide it up. The curtains of heavy plain woolen material are hung from just below the ceiling and reach right down to the floor.

184, 185   An elegant solution in a Paris attic flat whose changing rhythms of sloping roof and dormer windows has been taken up by the arrangement of the furniture. The smooth tops of the square side tables contrast well with the curved basket chairs. Comparable interrelations may be seen in the play with the lamp shades: the oval shape of the two suspended lamps in the corner is repeated by the horizontal oval of the counterweighted lamp above the dining table.

186

187

186, 187   This solution is larger in scale than previous examples of combined living-dining rooms. In the way it is divided up, however, it keeps within the range of feasibility offered by the simple rectangular room: sitting area and dining area face each other on the long axis. Furthermore, a principle is proclaimed here which we can recognize in many of the large-scale examples on the pages which follow: the living room is emphasized at the expense of the dining area in size as well as in the importance of its furniture. A long bench with a continuous frame and loose foam-rubber mattress lends an expansive air of comfort. The rectilinear shape of this arrangement is softened by tubular-steel easy chairs with shell-shaped seats of willow weave. A large dark carpet defines the living area. In contrast to this the dining area is reduced to a minimum: a wooden table, which like all good modern dining tables gives plenty of leg room, with a narrow frame under the top and legs which have been moved right to the corners, four wire-weave chairs, and a little sideboard the same height as the table. This small group is placed next to a balustrade behind which the staircase is hidden. An original effect is achieved by the picture above the staircase and the window strip above the bench; both are long rectangles, but the window opening with the thick foliage behind it looks like an abstract painting.

188

188, 189 In this example the rectangular main room is extended by a recess just large enough to accommodate a study corner with a bookcase. The main room has been divided into two almost equal areas: the dining area behind which a plain wall provides a neutral background, and the sitting area near the window with a small occasional table as its central feature. It is interesting to note how these two areas have been divided: the strip of floor between the two carpets is of exactly the same width as the tall picture whose dark surface cuts up the long white wall.

189

190

191

190   The center of gravity in this room is the fireplace wall, about which a sitting group has been loosely arranged. A black-and-red Persian rug links the two easy chairs on the left with the settee, which is placed at right angles to the wall to act as a room divider. Its importance is stressed by the vivid blue cover which makes it stand out against the other restrained colors. On the right, in the corner, is the dining area: gracefully elegant black-enameled wooden chairs with light woven seats and a circular table top of rosewood on a black metal frame. Behind it in the alcove are two shelves on which a few objets d'art are spaced out. The collector's pieces on the mantel (which has been extended in both directions) have been similarly laid out at random and set widely apart, so that each object shows up to full advantage against the white wall.

192

191   The door in the center of the rear wall divides up the horizontally stressed background of the room into areas of equal importance: on the left the dining area, on the right a leisure and reading corner with settee and radio. The areas are related to each other by a shelf wall, whose compartments are of the same width as the cupboards below them. The light shelves and white metal uprights stand out clearly from the blue-gray wall. This creates the impression that the room extends farther back behind the shelves. The narrow area in the foreground, marked off by a curtain, is the actual sitting room, with the painted peasant cupboard as its main feature.

192   The living area is a compact arrangement in front of the rear wall, towards which the boarded ceiling slopes down. The joints between the boards emphasize the impression of length. The room reaches forward in its entire length from the couch, which itself occupies the full width of the wall. A bookshelf has been ingeniously added to this zone, which is screened off from the dining area in the foreground by a cross-barrier of sideboards. Their backs serve as mounts for small temporary displays of photographs, posters and pictures. Below the window is a table top which acts as a working surface. Spherical lamps emphasize the various room areas.

193–196   In this carefully planned Swiss private house, with a succession of rooms strongly differentiated in character and height, the large combined living-dining room forms the center of the whole scheme. Turning left on entering one is confronted by the living area (193). The outer wall has been completely replaced by glass and offers a magnificent view over mountains and lake. A glass door leads to an outdoor terrace. As can be seen from the top lights, the ceiling rises toward the sitting area, which consists of a low table and light-weight easy chairs without arms, three of which have been pushed together to form a bench. On the far left a ramp can be discerned which leads up to the higher-lying sleeping quarters. The parents' bedroom adjoins the living room at the back. A sliding window between the two rooms can be opened so that the master of the house, who has his desk there, can join in the family activities in the living room. The bookshelves set into the parapet and the sloping wall of the ramp help to subdivide these large areas.

From the parents' bedroom, the eye travels over the living area to the dining recess (194) where the ceiling begins to rise in the opposite direction. The dining alcove is furnished with a round table, old chairs, and an old cupboard, which go well together. On the right of the dining area is the breakfast bar and the hatch to the kitchen.

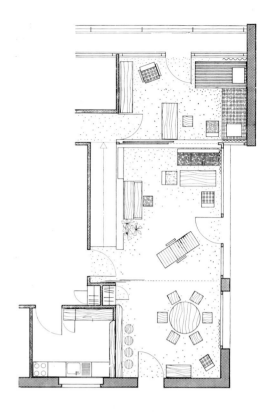

193

194

195, 196   The breakfast bar between kitchen and dining room can be shut off by a sliding door. A pivoting door on the left houses drinks and glasses on shelves fixed to its inside face. The doors are lined with a colored plastic laminate.

195

196

197

197   A generously proportioned and imposing room whose architecture and furniture are all of a piece. On the right-hand side is a long window wall, opposite a shelf and cabinet wall with vividly grained doors. A particularly interesting feature may be seen on the extreme left, where shelves are placed against a room-high window. The collector's pieces on their white boards stand out as silhouettes in front of the glass. Single shelves extend to the right as horizontal elements in front of the black rear wall, from which, conversely, light objects now stand out. In the background on the left is a desk and sitting area next to the cylindrical fireplace; in the foreground the dining area projects diagonally into the room.

198

199

198   The chimney, covered with polished travertine slabs, is the dividing element between living and dining areas. In the background of this very large room is the dining area, with sideboard units stretching from wall to wall, and a built-in cupboard wall incorporating a hatch and door into the kitchen. In the foreground, sofa and armchairs enclose the living area, whose other limits are the windowsill and hearth. Rectangular areas and block-like shapes characterize the general scheme of this room.

199   Great distinction and a strict sense of order are the first impressions made by this arrangement - an impression emanating from the long sideboard, the table parallel to it, and the sitting group at right angles, and also from the materials: choice veneers, chromium-plated steel, natural leather, and heavy velvet.

200

200–202   The combined living-dining room in the apartment of a New York architect and art collector shows how the utmost simplicity can result in the greatest refinement. From its layout to the choice of materials there is an artistically contrived sense of order. A sideboard was placed in the elongated rectangle as a room divider (201). This creates a narrow passage on the left, which leads into the room leading away from the door, while also defining the dining area. A natural-colored carpet of the same shade as the travertine slab floor provides a neutral background to the living area. The rectangular shape of the furniture has an important effect on its arrangement. Steel, leather, and marble are the predominant materials, and the white slabs provide an excellent background for setting off the sculptures. In accordance with their proportions, the large pictures were placed respectively to the right and left of the couch. The picture on the left, a Léger, catches the visitor's eye as he enters. Two small pictures are hung in line with the left edge of the settee to complete the restrained decorative treatment of the sitting area. In order not to disrupt the clear arrangement of the room by zones of light and shade, as single lamps would have done, all light was concentrated on the wall opposite the window, which thus acts as a large reflector. In addition, another strip light is sited over the dining table.

201

202

203

204

203, 204   This living-dining room, rebuilt by an Italian art collector from a fisherman's cottage on the Ligurian coast, combines old furniture and objets d'art of varying styles with modern fittings (shelves, fireplace) and mass-produced items (cane chairs, wall lights). Whitewashed walls, heavy ceiling beams, and a blue tiled floor form a rustic setting to which furniture and objets d'art have been added with a sure feeling for their individual worth. Though similar attempts elsewhere may only succeed in looking like a crowded antique shop, in this case a lively sitting room has been created by the use of modern techniques of interior decoration.

205   206

205, 206 The open rafterwork in the attic of an old Danish house provides a striking setting for a spacious living and dining room. The romantic aspect of this room has practical advantages as well, for the timber beams, far from constricting space, emphasize the airiness and height of the attic. Ledges and open compartments running along either side of the room provide space for sitting, display, and storage. The interplay of textures – rough-hewn wood, teak, plaster, and polished tiles – is the principal decoration. Here again living and dining areas are situated diagonally across from each other.

207

207-210 The problem of subdividing a long room into dining and living areas is solved in both these Scandinavian examples by a staircase to a lower floor that splits a story into two compartments. The stairwell and banister are a compulsory room-divider whose limits are underlined in one of the examples by the changed color of the floor covering. On the other hand, in both examples the banister has been kept thin and transparent; it is meant to suggest a boundary between the two areas rather than a solid demarcation. For the aesthetic model here is the undivided single room which springs from a desire for width and spaciousness. This is combined with a love of comfort in both cases.

209

210

207, 208 Dark plastic tiles outline the living area, which at the same time, however, is tied in with the other zone by the white fireplace wall. In the recess is a built-in book case, on the left the sitting area. The window surround is of wicker work. The dining area has very effective ventilation, for windows and doors provide a cross draft. The end wall is stressed horizontally by pictures hung in a row.

209, 210 Compared with the example on the left, much more color and texture (wallpaper, reed matting) have been used here. While this room is not as elongated, its layout is similar. Here the living area includes a work corner as well as fireplace and comfortable seats. Wallpaper and plate rack impart a rustic character to the dining area.

211

New opportunities for articulating a combined living-dining room arise from additions made to its plan. While the previous examples generally started out with a more or less elongated rectangle, the following pages illustrate examples in which an alcove opens out of a larger rectangular room to give an L-shaped arrangement.

The advantages of a room of this shape are obvious: more space, interesting intersections and views, opportunities for contrasts of light and dark, open and closed areas, color and texture. Because the functions of a living room require more space, the living area of an L-shaped room usually occupies the larger wing, while the dining area is nearly always situated in the alcove or shorter wing.

No matter how much their proportions and furniture may vary individually, one thing is common to all these examples: the kitchen is placed to make the angle of the L. This arrangement results quite naturally from the close relationship between dining area and kitchen, which open into each other through a hatch or a direct door.

212

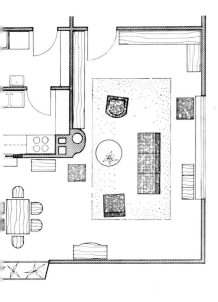

211, 212   A combined living-dining room with an L-shaped plan. The living area (212) has been characterized as the dominant zone by its carpet, which extends a good way beyond the cross wall of the dining room. It is further emphasized by such features as the book wall, the fireplace, and the door opposite the antique chest of drawers. Although these elements, apart from the chest, scarcely seem massive, the dining area (211) with its almost bare walls makes a much lighter impression. The upholstered chairs and stool near the fireplace are carefully matched in proportions and thanks to their light weight can be arranged in casual groups. Since the stool-shaped tables on the right by the window can be moved up to the chairs as required, new changes of layout are possible in the living area.

One wall of the dining alcove is taken up by a room-high plant window: the other two, apart from the hatch in the corner, have been kept as smooth uncluttered areas. The ideal picture of an unbroken wall has, however, been bought at the expense of omitting the door between dining room and kitchen, which, when there is nobody to pass things through the hatch, means walking a long way round through the living room. A good deal of the clear, stimulating effect that characterizes this example, of course, depends on the interplay of vividly - textured surfaces (bookcase, plant window) and unbroken wall areas in off-white.

213

214

215

213 The long living area on the left and the dining area on the right are connected in an L-shape. The adjoining kitchen was not closed off by solid walls but by a curtain and cupboard wall with an opening at eye level, an arrangement which allows the housewife to take a closer part in family affairs even though she may be at work in the kitchen. The cupboard compartments are accessible both from the kitchen and the living room; some doors are covered whith woven raffia.

214 In this example, which like example 213 is American, the living room extends the whole width of the house. It is surrounded by waist-high units of cabinets and shelves and in the center by a room-high fireplace and storage wall, so that it forms a closed block. The dining alcove is in a direct line with the fireplace and is connected with the kitchen through a serving hatch. Rare woods, narrow bricks, a light woolen carpet, and dark plastic tiles as the floor covering are the predominant materials.

215 A layout comprising hall, kitchen, dining recess, and sitting area, in which cubes and rectangular surfaces are closely related. This principle holds good throughout, from the tiled floor, the rectilinear armchairs, and the copper hood of the fireplace to the board-lined block of the kitchen wall. A door leads from the kitchen direct into the dining area.

216

The preceding examples illustrated two possibilities for dividing off living and dining areas: articulation by the placing of furniture and demarcation on the floor by carpets or coverings in contrasting colors or materials. The next four pages are devoted to examples in which the areas are vertically divided. The scale ranges from the application of shelves as room-dividers to the use of curtains, sliding doors, or folding partitions. The room-divider in the form of shelves is a special case, since it is intended merely to provide a form of demarcation, and not complete separation. Fig. 216 illustrates what is meant by this: seen from the dining area, the room-divider is a form of enclosure that does not completely obstruct the view into the living area. Room division is more or less marked according to the density of the objects on the shelves. Curtains, sliding doors, or folding partitions are a substitute for a solid wall; the curtain constitutes a visual barrier while the movable partitions provide acoustic isolation as well. Folding doors beyond a certain width, as illustrated in Fig. 217, are usually subdivided into several panels that can be pushed behind each other when open. In Fig. 218 an accordion-type plastic partition has been fitted so as to extend an existing cross wall; when pushed aside, the partitions occupy very little space.

217

218

219

220

In most cases it is enough to divide living and dining areas visually. If one prefers to set or clear the table without being seen from the living area, it is sufficient to draw a curtain – with a little care one can reduce rattling and clatter to a minimum. Cooking smells, however, can hardly be excluded by a curtain. Anyone who is fussy in this respect will prefer the collapsible partition. Under normal conditions however, it should be sufficient if smells are eliminated by cross-ventilation.

219, 220 Curtains are used as room-dividers in this Scandinavian house. The dining area communicates with the kitchen by a door. Fitting the curtain tracks behind a wooden cornice made all the curtains of the room look the same height. The large areas of textile provide attractive color contrasts.

221, 222 In this combined living-dining room in an old Italian apartment house, the dining recess is two steps above the living area. The first step has been stained black as a form of demarcation between two similar parquet floors, and the step is so broad that the upholstered seats of four individual chairs can be accommodated on it. As a visual screen five lengths of woven wood fiber have been used, each roughly the same width as the cushions. They run on ceiling tracks and can be pushed to one side.

221

222

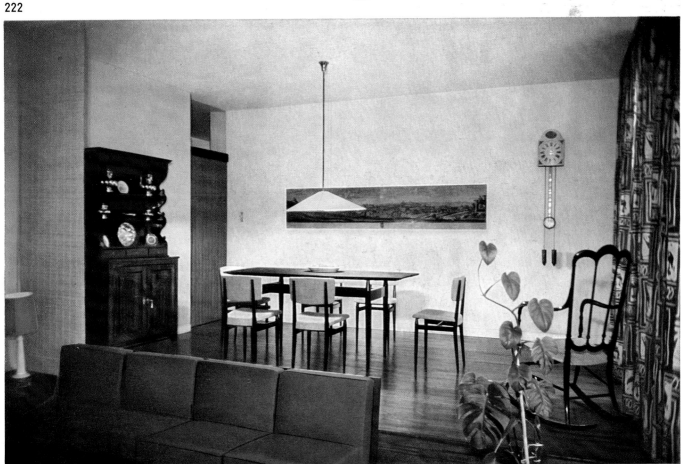

Many examples in this book show a striving for spaciousness and flexibility which might be taken as the hallmark of the modern style of living. Instead of a series of separate rooms, each of which served a single purpose only, such as dining room, library, and music room, nowadays we find a large multi-purpose room that can be subdivided to fulfil different functions. For the same overall size it provides a generously proportioned room, which can, however, be divided up into smaller areas and zones. Adaptability is the primary advantage of the open plan. The picture on the left illustrates this point. In the foreground the nursery is represented by a play table. A sliding door can shut this off from the next zone, which includes the dining area and the open kitchen alcove. A further means of separation is afforded by the curtain that runs across to the corner of the built-in cabinet: it marks the boundary of the living room, which can itself be further subdivided. The carefully planned system of circulation that determines the succession of areas creates an impression of spaciousness. The furniture has to fit in with this conception, as the vistas must not be obstructed by heavy or bulky pieces. Such storage space as is needed has therefore been confined to built-in units, lightweight shelves, and low chests of drawers. Incidentally it is no coincidence that the most interesting examples of the open plan originate from Scandinavia and North America, countries where life within the close family circle has become a matter of course and where at the same time there is a constant shortage of servants. If the housewife was not to be too cut off in her particular sphere of activity, kitchen, living room, and nursery had to be brought into a closer relationship.

The following pages also illustrate examples in which labor-saving problems and changes in social status are only secondary considerations, examples which have chiefly arisen from a desire to lay out extensive parts of an apartment or house as a continuous succession of rooms. The equipment of each individual room is also influenced by considerations which can only be understood in relation to its part in the whole scheme. Contrasts are most important in this respect: in the atmosphere of the room, the color scheme, the alternation of light and dark zones, narrow areas with wide ones, and the stimulation evoked by the use of contrasting materials and textures. In addition, there are the sudden surprises afforded by an unexpected view or a sudden change of direction. The opportunities for such contrasts increase in proportion to the size of the rooms. As individual examples prove, how-ever, exciting layouts can be created in ordinary apartments too.

Conditions are particularly favorable if such aspects can be planned in advance when building one's own home. In addition to the foregoing design features are the effects contributed by the architectural frame itself, such as changes in ceiling height, split-level floors, or the alternation of solid and void in wall surfaces. The two-story living hall is indisputably the most im-pressive feature, since a layout that is suddenly extended vertically trans-mits a completely new sensation of space. A two-story room is often em-bellished with the further attraction provided by a gallery: from its height the living room is seen in quite a new perspective, a piece of visual excitement which often accounts for this story being extended to accommodate a study and library.

224

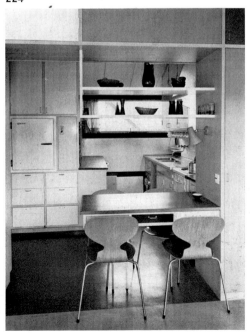

Figs. 223 and 224 are described on page 153.

225

226

227

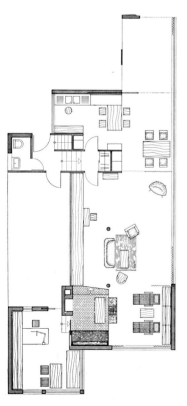

223–227 The arrangement and furnishing of this Danish house provide an ideal example of the open plan. Despite the spacious effect of this room its area is no greater than that of a small two-story house. The layout develops lengthwise along the south wall, which has been dissolved completely by windows and sliding glass doors. The nursery adjoins the bedroom, not illustrated here (226, blue wall in the far background); towards the window is the open play room, and next to it two small bedrooms (416). Next come the kitchen and dining area (223, 224). Apart from the breakfast table and shelf unit suspended from the ceiling and forming a small barrier, the kitchen is open toward the surrounding rooms: the housewife can thus keep the children's play area constantly under supervision while attending to her kitchen chores. The dining area with its old furniture is just a few steps away. The whole suite of rooms as far as the bedroom at the back has a cabinet wall on the inside, extending up to roof level, which provides a wealth of storage space behind a battery of doors painted different colors. The living room (226) is almost twice as long as it is wide. The series of windows above the lower range of cabinets provides light at a lower level for the architect-owner's drafting office. A sitting area with a red divan leads to the fireplace corner two steps lower down (225), which is faced with light-colored bricks. Next to the couch, on a brick base, is the door to the owner's office. At the upper level (227) a reading corner adjoins the built-in library shelves. The end wall features a window and door leading to a pergola-roofed terrace.

228

229

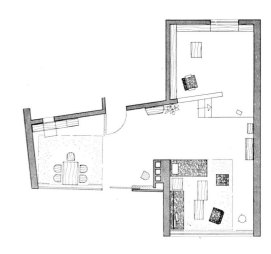

230

228-230   The disposition of this layout is determined partly by the sloping site that commands a beautiful view, and partly by a desire to ensure different and exciting shapes for the various zones. From the hall a door (228 right) leads into a virtually unfurnished anteroom which leads the eye immediately to the large picture window and the terrace door (229, right). The dining area is situated on the right and can be shut off by a curtain, while the table has been moved right up to the window wall. To make the room appear longer, the far wall has been painted a dark color; on the right, a hatch leading into the kitchen has been fitted into a cupboard reaching half the height of the room. From the dining recess the living area appears as a polygon (230): in front on the right a short partition wall punctuates the view; on the left a Baroque chest of drawers catches the eye. Farther along a short parapet juts out and three steps lead up to the library. Finally a free-standing sculpture of a madonna stands on the landing next to an intarsia-work cupboard, all of which register as three-dimensional accents leading to the living area (229). Here the seating is so arranged that both couches command fine views over the city.

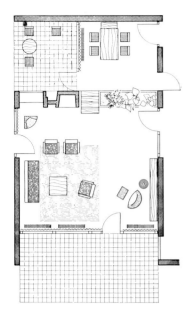

231

232

233

231–233 Like the preceding example, this layout has also been divided up by a split-level arrangement: the dining area (233) is five steps higher than the living area and is supplemented by a roofed terrace on the same level. Another exciting feature is the sloping roof lined with larch boarding. The fireplace, built of rough-hewn stone, dominates the center of the room; it has a second aperture at the back, facing the sitting area. The dining area, with a door into the kitchen, is divided off from the living area by a handrail and a wooden plant trough. Also, a bookcase stands to the left of the fireplace (231), and behind it a glass wall reveals the terrace outside. The front of the room affords ample room for a sitting area. As in the previous example, the floor consists of polished stone slabs. Since the window goes right down to the floor without a window ledge, the radiators stand out in relief, a solution better than unsuccessful attempts at hiding them behind trellis-work grilles.

234

235

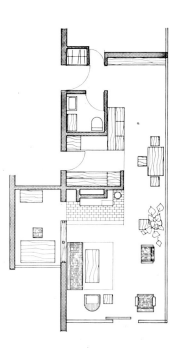

236

234–237 The hall, dining area, living room, and study of this Danish bunga-low are arranged in succession around a central core consisting of a bath-room, kitchen, and fireplace. On entering the hall one is confronted by the blank bathroom wall on the right, the bedroom door on the left, and a bookcase (235, right background). From here one gets a view from the dining recess to the wider living area along the longitudinal axis of the house (236). The side wall of brick and plate glass windows emphasizes the length of the room. At the end of the room a sliding door in the glass wall leads into the garden. The dining area in the foreground is only a few steps away from the kitchen, which is situated in the central core. Exactly opposite the dining table are the built-in kitchen cabinets, which continue around the corner. The sitting area (237), with its unusual combination of cane chair, teak table, sofa, and boldly patterned rugs, has a picturesque character. Its rear wall, which continues to enclose the garden outside, has an open book-case built on to it at the right (234). Next to the bookcase one steps down to the study which has a desk by the window and a bureau on the inside wall. The fireplace wall, consisting of several intersecting rectangular shapes (235), is the main focus. The continuity of the open room is stressed by the use of the same materials throughout: creosoted timber, natural or white-washed bricks on the walls, and darker bricks on the floor.

237

238–242   Hall, dining area, and living room flow into each other in this Italian example, whose arrangement is meant to spotlight the individual object. For example, in the hall (238), the ceiling is white, and the floor consists of light marble slabs; the wall is covered with a dark fabric which acts as a foil for a Baroque statue of a putto and an elegantly shaped cane chair. In the background a wall of woven wooden slats is suspended from the ceiling. This screen has been successfully exploited to provide an element in the articulation of space, and thanks to its transparency, the outlines of the living room may be recognized; on the other hand, it is dense enough to serve as a backdrop for the peasant chest, the china fruit bowl, and the asymmetrically hung portrait of a woman in the hall. The choice and arrangement of these objects display a confident sense of proportion. The separate anteroom opens into the dining area (242), which stands out from the marble floor like an island on account of its circular mat. The living area is outlined by a dark pile carpet (239, 240). A door opening on the right of the fireplace has been transformed into a built-in book case. On the left, a glass case displays three guitars as silhouetted features. This talent for imaginative decoration is also revealed in the sliding doors of the built-in cabinet, which are painted in contrasting colors.

238

239

240

241

242

243

This suite in a New York apartment house might equally well be found in Brussels, Milan, or Zurich. The furniture embodies an international trend in the modern style of living that has been developing for over a quarter of a century and is now so clearly recognizable that national differences hardly carry any weight. What is particularly characteristic of this furniture is the clear cubic shape and the stress on structural honesty. This means that the structure of a piece of furniture is not regarded as a support that should be concealed, but as an integral part that contributes substantially to the design. As far as materials are concerned, this conviction has encouraged the use of steel in furniture construction. Today, square steel tubes, round bars, and plastic are as acceptable as the finest mahogany. A preference for rectangular shapes and clearly visible articulation is equally important in the field of room design. Furniture is laid out on strictly geometrical lines which, as far as possible, should not be disturbed.

244

243–245   In order to provide wall space for a couch (243) the short cross wall at the entrance was extended to twice its width by a woven slat screen. The edges of the screen are bound with metal so that it can be pulled sideways easily. To the left stands a built-in cabinet, whose dark-blue doors with white borders punctuate the wall surface strongly. Like all dark wall areas, these doors seem to enlarge the room by appearing distant. On entering, the eye first glimpses the right-hand wall (244), whose length is emphasized by a low sideboard. In front of this, a passage leads to the two cabinet units below the window. This passage is confined toward the room center by two leather chairs placed side by side (243). A stool of the same design and a square glass-topped table, all with chromium-plated legs, stand in front of the black-framed fireplace. Together with the dark-blue couch, they form a sitting area in front of the screen. A second sitting area is provided by the long, four-part upholstered bench below the window (245)

245

and the two casual tables in front of it. This is directly opposite the dark couch, the focal point of the first group. Such corresponding relations of function, size, and area are characteristic of the design of this room. A similar relationship exists, for example, between the fireplace and the sideboard along the facing wall (244). The picture above illustrates another general principle: nowhere in the room is the wall hidden by pieces of tall furniture. The cupboard units on the right, the bench, fireplace, and the chairs in the foreground are all approximately the same height. The resulting impression of spaciousness contributes greatly to the character of the room. The color scheme sets off the shades of the fabrics and leather covers against the off-white of the walls and the pastel gray of the carpet. The window bench and the plain curtains match the light colors of the room. Vivid contrasts are provided by colored cushions, flowers, and accessories. The abstract pictures and the plants have been consciously drawn into the scheme.

246 The dining room of the New York apartment illustrated on the three preceding pages, compared with the impressive living room, has a more intimate character. The walnut cabinets of the sideboard are suspended from the wall, as are the bookshelves above. Cane and bentwood armchairs stand around a table with cherrywood top and white metal frame. The colors are warm and bright. The coarse weave of the floor covering looks well in this informal room, whose height appears extended by vertically striped curtains.

246

247

248

249

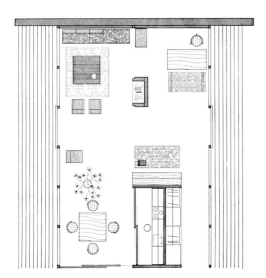

247–249 The structural shape and furniture of this bungalow, which a Danish architect has built for himself at Öresund, were inspired by Japanese examples. The light and elegant beam construction and the Japanese modular system, as applied to the beams, walls, windows, and sliding doors, underline this effect. The sparse, severe furniture is in keeping with the over-all restraint and simplicity. The plan demonstrates how the architect applied the principles of the open plan to achieve flowing space. A solid core with bath and kitchen stands at one end of a large rectangular room with glass window walls on both long sides. Open living has a double meaning here: the rooms are open to one another, and the house itself is open to nature, especially on the side facing the sea (248). The same picture also illustrates the core: on the left at the back, a dark cabinet wall with a door to the bathroom; nearer to the front, closed off by two sliding doors, the kitchen, which is so tiny that there is room at the back (see plan) for further cupboards; at the front wall of the core there is a book wall with suspended cabinets. In the surrounding zone, the bedroom faces the beach and its sliding door remains open all day (248). The dining area is located by the kitchen. The living room, which extends the full width of the house, is divided by the free-standing whitewashed fireplace into a sitting area (247), and a study for the owner of the house (249). A dark-stained timber wall provides a neutral background for both zones and silhouettes the furniture. Elegance of shape and linear patterns of light and shade characterize the few choice pieces of furniture. For the sake of aesthetic unity, curtains have been replaced by roller blinds of the woven slat type. The sea chest next to the couch contains a radio and record player, while the loudspeaker has been mounted behind a circular fabric-covered aperture in the rear wall.

250

250-254   This house in Munich, whose living and dining rooms are illustrated on the following four pages, has such amply proportioned, tall rooms that the architectural frame can incorporate every kind of feature: change of ceiling height, alcoves, a gallery, and contrasts of textures, lights and darks, solids and voids. In addition there is excitement provided by the furniture: the ingenuous character of some elements recalling a Bavarian farmhouse contrasting with the worldly elegance of the Italian pieces. The unlikely combination heightens the charm of the one style and the refinement of the other.

152

250–252 The main room, which extends through two stories, overlooks the garden through an extraordinarily large window-wall. In the end wall (250), a doorway leads to the bedrooms on the left. Above, from a vantage point on the stairs protected by a white railing, one can look down into the living room. The fireplace, built against the stairwell, has a flue shaped like an obelisk. In a paneled alcove next to the fireplace, a couch and three curved armchairs constitute a friendly sitting area.

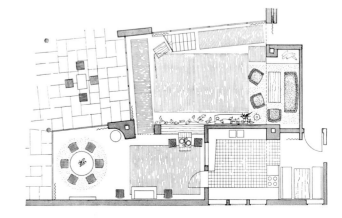

252

On the right, shelves house a collection of handicraft items; beneath the chairs lies a white sheepskin rug. The painted peasant cupboard dominates the long inner wall, and above it, at the same level as the upper edge of the paneling in the sitting alcove, the boarded ceiling begins. The wooden floor is covered with one large and several small patchwork rugs.

On the other short side of the living room (251), a mezzanine floor with bookshelves has been inserted. Below, garden seats are visible through the glass wall. The television set below the stairs can be watched from the alcove diagonally across the room. The recess next to the peasant cupboard (252) gives on to the adjoining quarters: above the free-standing radiator are open shelves which provide a view into the next room. As this section is regarded merely as a passage to the dining room, it has no windows. It receives sufficient light from the neighboring rooms and has purposely been left slightly dark to contrast with the dining room, which receives ample light through its two glass walls.

253

254

253–254 The dining room in the glass porch consists of a round table with lightweight Italian olivewood chairs. The circular shape of the table and carpet is repeated by the portly old iron stove, which has been chosen as a counterpoint to the elegant dining furniture. The silhouette of the stove stands out handsomely against the white plaster wall. In the passage behind the open shelves is a breakfast bar with high stools; beyond this a hatch and door lead into the kitchen.

255

256

257

258

259

A new conception of space and more abundant possibilities for design present themselves when the center of the house has been built as a two-story hall. The examples shown here are extremely spacious, but even in a smaller area it can be both practically and aesthetically advantageous to extend part of the living room through two stories. Whether the house is large or small, the same stimulating effects may be achieved by contrasting high and low, narrow and wide, and light and dark room areas.

In this house in Brussels (255–257), the library and study are situated on the gallery. The long room below the gallery is the dining room, marked off from the living room by a sideboard placed at right angles to the wall. As the couch in the main part runs at right angles too, it was possible to place additional seats between the two room-dividers. The enormous Scandinavian room (258-259) has been arranged more casually. Several sitting areas are dotted here and there over the room, their orientation towards focal points such as the open hearth being quite incidental. The impression of luxury is reinforced by the tropical winter garden.

260

260   A dining room in an old building, whose extreme loftiness is somewhat relieved by the large chandelier and the long marble relief. Although not particularly big, this room seems surprisingly extensive with its sparse furniture: the round table and the classic bentwood chairs of the last century. In contrast to the combined living-dining room arrangement, other room areas did not have to be considered here; hence the table group could be made the dominant feature in the center of the room. The fireplace and a few objets d'art and collector's pieces increase the elegant effect.

Dining room and dining area

Dining room and dining area

261 A dining area in the hall offers the advantage of a convenient place for eating that does not encroach on the living room.

261

If the material in this book had been assembled a decade earlier, the traditionally separate dining room would have taken up much more space than it has here. Only in the last few years has the practice of dispensing with a separate dining room, even where there is plenty of space, gained wide acceptance. The reasons, whether the international trend toward a spacious open plan or simply shortage of room and lack of domestic help, have already been discussed in the previous chapter on the combined living-dining room.

Despite the current preference for the open plan, the separate dining room still has its advocates today. For practical and aesthetic reasons they prefer to dine in a separate room with no direct connection with the living room. They enjoy the element of surprise on leading a guest to the festive table in a new setting, and after a meal they want to be able to go back into the living room, where neither food smells nor the clattering of dishes annoy them. In their living room they want comfortable seats, a fireplace, their books, and perhaps a desk, but no dining table. And they are convinced that it is not only more sensible but also simpler to furnish two separate rooms individually than to harmonize two areas in one combined room. Whatever one may feel with regard to these arguments, a personal decision must be made, and nothing would be more inept than to call advocates of the separate dining room old-fashioned.

No matter whether one wishes to achieve a formal effect in a large dining room or prefers to stress intimacy in a smaller one, the necessary furniture can be kept to a minimum: dining table and chairs, and some kind of sideboard or serving table. Anything beyond this depends on the size of the room and the style which each individual likes best.

Like so many other good ideas, a compromise solution comes from Scandinavia, which does not require a separate room for eating and yet provides a separate place for it that disturbs neither living room nor kitchen. By this plan a hall or mezzanine can be furnished as a living area (264–267). Where existing conditions prevent one from putting this solution into effect, a combination of dining area and kitchen may be arranged, as illustrated on pages 178–195.

262

262   This is a good example of a sumptuous way to furnish a dining room. The formal character of the room is softened by the plant window just visible on the left. The effect of the large wall surfaces is not disturbed by pictures. Clock and mirror in matching shapes and both gilded are the only decorative features. A sideboard was not necessary as the kitchen is close by.

263

263 This bright room, overlooking the garden, was furnished with the utmost restraint. The large plant window is lighted at night by an illuminated panel in the ceiling and provides a decorative background. As the appearance of the room is enhanced by the large wall areas, a hanging lamp might have spoiled the effect; hence the light was fixed close to the ceiling. The floor of French marble slabs contributes greatly to the elegance of the room. The shell-shaped upholstered chairs on tubular steel legs give a light appearance to the table group and enliven it with the different colors of their upholstery. The sideboard suspended from the wall, with its solid unbroken form, acts as a counterpoint to the airy volume of the room.

264

265

264-267 The pictures on these two pages give some indications as to how a passage or connecting room can be transformed into a dining room. Thus a useless corner in a Swedish house (264) was turned into a cozy room by sheer inventiveness and courage in the use of color. The difficulties which arose due to the inadequacies of the room – a cellar with tiny basement windows, low ceiling, and steep staircase – have been wonderfully overcome by the aid of color. The windows were made into decorative features by the insertion of colored panes. The low ceiling with its painted beams contributes to the intimacy of the room. Stairs, chairs, and window frames in the same shade of blue are important components of the color scheme, to which lamps, plate rack, basket, and spinning wheel act as further decorative features. The Danish house (265) is considerably simpler in its furniture. Here the dining room was situated on the mezzanine landing in front of a big window. The china cupboard opposite the kitchen door also serves as a counter.

266, 267   A dining hall which can be furnished in different ways. This small dining area for four people was accommodated below the window next to the kitchen door. For special occasions, the table is moved into the middle of the room, and the large leaves at the narrow ends of the table are extended to seat ten people.

266

267

268

268   Spacious living in an American kitchen, with a central dining area and adjoining living zone that can be extended through the use of the sitting and dining area on the veranda. The dining table is on casters and has a plastic top so that it can also be used as a working surface in the kitchen. It is normally pushed under a shelf unit, which serves as a sideboard and has been built in to act as a room divider. The U-shaped living area is used for everyday activities apart from the main living room, which is not shown. The two divans can be made up into spare beds.

Practical considerations are paramount when dining room and kitchen are combined, but this need not mean that the dining area must become merely an extension of the kitchen. There are many ways of arranging the furniture to give the dining area a distinctive character in its surroundings.

The most difficult problem is undoubtedly the dining-kitchen. When the kitchen surrounds the dining table on all sides, the only way to distinguish it is by the art of laying the table, the choice of the china, or a few flowers. In the evening, a hanging lamp with a low shade can limit the illumination to the table so that stove and sink are in darkness during the meal.

The situation is more favorable when the shape of the kitchen is such that the dining area can be located by a window (293). In this way it is still a direct part of the kitchen, but is sufficiently far away to allow its area to be defined by different-colored walls or wallpapers, and by putting up pictures, shelves, or curtains.

Another frequently employed solution is to have the dining area and kitchen in one room, but to divide it up by grouping the furniture (269) or using built-in units (277) and curtains (278) to create two different zones. This is what we call a dining area outside the kitchen; an ante room or an alcove of the living room has been made into a dining area separated from the kitchen by a cupboard wall with a large serving hatch and a connecting door (273). This door is often a sliding one that is generally left open, while the size of the hatch allows a view of the neighboring room. Kitchen and dining area are thereby closely connected. This layout is motivated not only by the practical consideration of saving steps for the housewife in a servantless age, but also by the intention to create large, inter connected rooms in the spirit of the open plan. This idea also accounts for the endeavor that is made to design a kitchen and dining area in harmony with one another. This can be effected by a unified color scheme (273, 275) or by the use of similar wood for the furniture of both areas (271). Nowadays water-repellent teak is often used; it has long proved its suitability in the kitchen as a material for drainboards. It will thus be seen that an attempt is made to separate the two zones when the dining area is in the kitchen and to link them up when it is just outside the kitchen.

No such considerations arise about the so-called breakfast area, which is less demanding in both space and equipment. It functions as a cheerful spot in which to drink a cup of coffee or eat a snack, and that is why practical, space-saving furniture is important. It does not need to be distinguished from its surroundings. Fig. 288 demonstrates the possibilities of producing original and bright breakfast areas, where the informal atmosphere of the kitchen can be exploited to produce playful and amusing arrangements.

269

270

In the following pages we see plans that combine the kitchen and dining area in one room (269–272) and other examples in which the dining area is visually separated from the kitchen by cabinet walls (273–276) The first four examples start with the same data: an elongated rectangular room is half taken up by a U-shaped kitchen area, with a large expanse of window on one wall. A central cabinet, which serves both as a working surface and as a sideboard, divides the kitchen from the dining area. Thanks to this space-saving double function, even such a tiny corner as in Fig. 270 can still be utilized as a dining area. The lamp suspended above the dining table also serves a double purpose: it provides glare-free light and lends a more elegant touch that clearly distinguishes the dining area from the working zone of the kitchen.

269   The U-shaped kitchen is linked to the dining area by a wall of cabinets with brightly painted sliding doors. The broiler and food storage shelf are set into the rear wall at eye level. A built-in ceiling light illuminates both stove and refrigerator. When it is dark, the working area is also illuminated by strip lights above stove and sink. Above the dining area hangs a lamp with a bell-shaped metal shade. Kitchen and dining area can be divided off from the living room by a sliding door.

271

272

270   The narrow space in front of the kitchen has been used to the best advantage by building in a bench and a fixed table. The table top is attached to the wall and supported by a single metal column to give the people sitting there as much leg room as possible. This is particularly important as the bench cannot be pushed back like the chairs. The telephone extension in the kitchen is very useful as it eliminates the necessity of going back and forth to the main telephone in the hall or living room.

271   In this and the following example, the division between kitchen and dining area is emphasized by the installation of a hanging cupboard. Here it is located over the sink and serves to store china; the sliding doors can be opened on either side.

272   To stress the more formal character of the dining area, the back of the hanging cupboard has been painted a dark color, and the lower cupboard has been faced with veneer. As in Figs. 269 and 270, one compartment of the lower cupboard opens to the dining table; it is used to keep napkins, tablecloths and items of a similar nature.

273

274

273 Similar shades of timber and identically colored floor coverings in the kitchen and dining area. The large hatch can be closed by a roller shutter of wooden slats which runs from side to side. The semicircular counter projects so far into the kitchen that it provides a comfortable breakfast table for four. There are wall cupboards with access from both sides above and below the hatch. As the entrance on the right is usually kept open, a sliding door is more useful than a hinged one, which, when open, would project into one of the rooms.

274 Kitchen and dining area are separated by a cupboard reaching almost up to the ceiling, and a correspondingly high screen of woven slats in a wooden frame in the foreground. The hatch also serves as a breakfast counter.

Despite the dividing cupboard wall, kitchen and dining area in all these cases have been designed to harmonize through the repetition of color and material (273, 275), through the functional links of door and hatch, and through cupboard compartments accessible from both sides. The special nature of these examples becomes apparent when compared to the ordinary living-dining room, where the connection between dining room and kitchen is less marked and as a rule merely consists of a small hatch (211) or a door in an otherwise uninterrupted wall (219).

275

276

275   The use of dark horizontal and vertical areas and the alternation of yellow and reddish panels are common to both kitchen and dining area. The tones of the woodwork are also repeated in the wall color on the left. A shelf unit for glasses and vases closed only by sliding glass doors is in conformity with the intention of having an open wall.

276   A cheerful example where the wallpaper of the dining area has been continued in the kitchen. As in all these examples the handles of the upper cupboards, which open to both rooms, are fixed within easy reach.

277

277-280 Where kitchen and dining area adjoin, it is a question of choice how far the two areas are to be separated visually. The open or half-open examples (269–272) require careful planning to avoid the appearance of a messy kitchen during the meal. Usually a sliding door, screen, or blind can be fitted across any hatches or openings to close off the cooking area when necessary. These examples show some further methods of partitioning. The simplest kind of partition is a curtain (278), which is suitable where the kitchen is lighted from the dining area. Where the ceiling is divided into two equal parts by a beam, there is an obvious place from which to hang the curtain. The narrow passage next to the stove can also be curtained off so that the kitchen is completely separate and shut off from view.

Apart from curtain fabric, plastic sheeting can be used for the curtain. Even woven slats, which occur often as a lively decorative material in our illustrations, may be employed. This is exemplified in a French country house (279, 280), where the kitchen cupboards are hidden by a blind.

Finally, there is another solution with built-in cupboards. The large kitchen and dining room in an American house (277) was divided by a 6 foot cupboard wall, with wooden sliding doors in the lower cupboards and glass ones in the upper range to show off the china as a decorative feature.

278

279

280

In larger households it has become more and more common to install an additional breakfast area apart from the actual dining room. It can serve at any time of the day as a temporary snack counter (281). Here the children can be given their meals quickly, or a snack can be eaten late at night. The improvised character of most breakfast areas is indicated by the fact that the table top is often a flap or folding leaf.

The term 'breakfast bar' which is often employed for this practical idea (282) is justified not only because the general idea of a bar is carried over (with all the chairs in line and the server on the other side) but is also due to the fact that the chairs, like bar stools, often have particularly tall legs. While the normal height of a dining table is 28″ to 29½″, the height of kitchen cabinets whose counter tops are used as working surfaces runs from 31½″ to 35½″. If one is to breakfast at one of these cupboard units, the chair must be higher than normal.

281

282

281   A breakfast alcove by the hatch. This simple solution is possible wherever the top of the counter projects sufficiently far forward. As the hatch is of normal table height, ordinary chairs can be used. The white wall strip beneath the counter should, however, be painted with a tough washable paint.

282   Breakfast bar in an American kitchen. At the same height as the stove and sink and at right angles to them runs a cupboard with a projecting plastic top; in front of it stand two bar stools. As in Fig. 281, this breakfast area is in front of the kitchen proper, which is an advantage when there are children.

283

283   Breakfast area in the kitchen of a Californian patio house. Because of
the warm climate, meals are often taken in the open at the round table in
the inner courtyard, which explains why a hatch has been built into the
window wall below the blue enameled cupboards. The breakfast area runs
at right angles to a sideboard six inches higher -- an example of the difference
between working top and normal table height. The table, covered with
patterned plastic tiles, is fixed to the wall, while the other end is supported
by a single column in order to leave plenty of leg room. The kitchen telephone above the table on the window wall is very useful.

284

284 A particularly successful example of a breakfast bar in an American household. The kitchen has been partitioned off from the dining area a little further to the right (not visible here) by a block of cupboard units into which the electric stove has been built. On the back of this block, wooden shelves can be pulled out at the right height for the three children. The mother uses the table tops on either side of the stove as a sideboard and can thus keep her eye on the children all the time. The top cupboard suspended from the ceiling can be opened from either side and contains the china in daily use. The whole kitchen can be closed to the dining room by a sliding wall whose timber-framed paper panels (left) are a reminder of the Japanese origin of the family.

285 The breakfast area in the previous examples lay outside the kitchen proper; we now have a number of examples where its position is more central. In this Swedish kitchen a shelf between two cabinets extends to form a breakfast table. The trapezoid shape of the plastic covered table top looks less unwieldy than a rectangle. The stool backrests are low to avoid a cluttered appearance. The table area is accentuated by picture tiles set into the white-tiled rear wall. Strip lights fixed at regular intervals below the wall cupboards supply the necessary illumination.

285

286

286   The table top next to the electric stove serves as a working surface and breakfast area. To gain leg room, the cupboard in this area has been reduced to a narrow base. Here, as in Fig. 284, stove, sideboard, and breakfast area are grouped within easy reach. A ventilator in the ceiling draws off cooking smells. Through the window the mother has an uninterrupted view of the charming little playground.

287, 288   These two breakfast areas were both fitted successfully into a minimum of space, but the solution of similar problems could hardly be more different. In each case only two people can be accomodated. In the first example (287) this results in a cool functional solution, which derives a surrealist touch from the female face on the Italian ceramic plate and a cheerful atmosphere from the two-color glass lamp. The other example (288) is of a personal, amiable group, which proves its owner a passionate collector. In the informal atmosphere of his kitchen he gave his whimsy full rein. An old café table, an ornate bentwood chair, and a turned stool make up the movable pieces, while on the shelves we see baskets, colored jugs, bottles, and dishes of the most diverse shapes. Modern china on the same shelves show that these pieces do not lead a museum existence but are in constant use. The whole collection is exhibited on thin glass shelves, which avoid stressing the horizontality of each level and emphasize instead the unity of the wall.

287

288

289

289 This dining area in the kitchen, which introduces a series of similar examples, demonstrates the attempt to give an individual and personal atmosphere to the technically perfected world of the kitchen. The steel cabinet stands quite unselfconsciously opposite the painted cupboard, and the modern chairs harmonize with the old gate-leg table, which can be reduced in size by folding back the frame. The copper casserole on the cupboard, the wall rack for silver spoons, and the faience tiles all fit in, as do the cane stand with toys and the copper lamp shade.

The 'dining kitchen' is a compromise compared to the examples in which the dining area is outside the kitchen or at least on its periphery. This compromise can work only if another dining room is available for entertaining. In contrast to the breakfast area with its specially informal and improvised character, the dining area is an important place. For special occasions it should have a more comfortable setting than can be provided in the kitchen. But even where the dining area in the kitchen serves for every day, its arrangement and equipment must be very carefully planned. The most suitable arrangement seems to be that in examples 293 and 294 where the dining area has been moved toward the window; it is particularly good if the dining area has its own door (294). More difficult is the situation illustrated below (290), where the kitchen cabinets have been extended in a long line on the right as far as the window. In this case an attempt has been made to distinguish the wall alcove from the kitchen by painting it a dark color and creating a contrasting atmosphere by details like the frilled curtains and the counter balanced lamp.

290

291

292

291   In this Swedish example, the everyday dining area is in the kitchen and the formal dining area in the combined living-dining room next to the kitchen. A window-like opening serves as a hatch, with colorful peasant decorations on the shutters and frame.

292   A Danish kitchen, where the meals are taken at a table on a light tubular-steel frame with a dark scratch-proof top. Two end flaps can be put up for additional space, and thanks to its light weight, the table can easily be pulled out and turned around. The box unit next to it has a hinged door, which conceals compartments for napkins, place mats, and other necessities.

293

293   In this elongated and comparatively narrow kitchen, the equipment has been kept to the walls at the front of the room, so that its whole width at the back can be used as a dining area. The room is entered by a door on the left whose frame is just visible on the picture. The housewife has only two or three steps between the stove and the table, whose light top and bentwood frame contrasts well with the turquoise-blue armchairs.

294

295

294, 295 The layout in this example is similar to the previous one except that the kitchen is somewhat broader, which gives more room to move about in the dining area. The table has been drawn up in front of the window on the right (295) and it was therefore possible to install a sewing unit along the end wall. An attempt has been made by the most varied means (wallpaper, curtains, pictures, lamp) to stress the comfort of the dining area as compared with the green and white of the kitchen. The drawer units of the sewing table, however, repeat the color scheme of the kitchen cabinets, and teak table tops are common to both areas. The boarded ceiling running crosswise, also painted green, counteracts the tunnel-like character of the room.

296

296 A two-sided glass-walled cupboard connects the dining room and kitchen, so that crockery can be reached from either side. A serving hatch opens below at the level of the working surfaces.

The kitchen

The kitchen

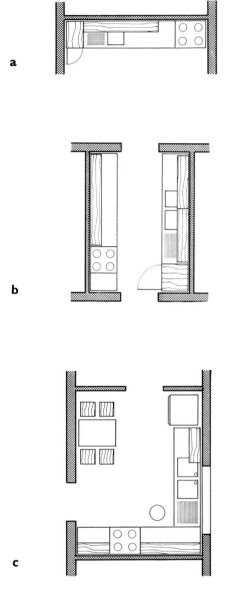

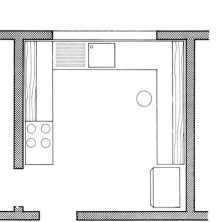

The amount of time needed for housework can be considerably cut down by a practical arrangement of the kitchen, where the housewife spends the largest proportion of her working time. Counter tops at the correct height should be related to each other so as to provide an uninterrupted flow of operations. Dust-free storage of utensils and food, easily cleaned and durable kitchen equipment, suitable lighting of the working surfaces, and adequate ventilation are matters of primary consideration in kitchen design.

These requirements have resulted in similar solutions in nearly all countries and have led to the production of standardized furniture. The outsized kitchen of former days has disappeared and in its place we have a compact area efficiently designed for working and sometimes for dining as well. It consists generally of variable built-in units, grouped horizontally. Floor and wall cabinets, the wall units of shallower depth, are separate. The tops of the floor cabinets make up large continuous working surfaces, so that the traditional kitchen table in the middle of the room can be dispensed with and the housewife's journeys from one side of the room to the other can be shortened. Stove, refrigerator, and sink are built-in together to provide a single surface covered with stainless steel or plastic.

A few plans have proved particularly practical. For very small households the single-line arrangement is recommended, with stove, working surface, and sink next to each other (scheme *a*). The working surface should be at least two feet square, with a height of 31″ to 35″ for standing work, and approximately 26″ for that done sitting. The double-line kitchen (scheme *b*) results when the side opposite the entrance has a second door, possibly leading to the dining area. Stove and working surface can then be on one long wall, sink, refrigerator, and storage cabinets on the other. The L-shaped plan (scheme *c*), where the working surfaces are at right angles to each other, gives a free corner where a dining area may be arranged; access to the table and through traffic need not interfere with circulation while meals are being prepared. For large kitchens the U-shaped plan (scheme *d*) is suitable. It is comparable to the two-line kitchen but has another working surface below the window. The housewife has uninterrupted space to move around and large continuous working surfaces; wasted space in the corners can be avoided by installing cabinets.

In addition there are a number of useful devices such as built-in refrigerators and stoves, broilers within easy reach, cupboards specially designed to hold appliances, automatic garbage disposal units, rotating shelves for more convenient storage, and retractable table tops for sit-down jobs. The surfaces of the built-in units are covered with a plastic laminate which is acid-proof and scratch-resistant. Veneers of suitable wood, such as teak, are also used. Floors should be easy to clean, unslippery, and quiet. Suitable floor coverings include tiles and slabs, cork, linoleum, and plastic, as well as the traditional wood floors, sealed in this case with synthetic resin.

However justified the demands for hygiene and rational planning may be, the kitchen is not meant to be a technical laboratory. Color can contribute much to relieve the sober, functional character of many ultra-modern kitchens. Hence, in addition to the usual white, light pastel colors are now available as well as the warm tones of wood veneers and a few brilliant color accents. In some unorthodox American designs (315, 316) an attempt has been made to put the stove back in the center of the room, where it used to be for many centuries.

297

297, 298 This French example is distinguished by its definite color accents. The background is white, which suggests cleanliness. Working surfaces are of gray-blue plastic; the tiled floor and facing are kept pastel gray. Against these neutral or cool colors some cupboard doors are a brilliant corn yellow with inside surfaces of bright red. The recess for spice containers is lined with rosewood.

299 The frequently tiny working kitchen demands the utmost exploitation of the space available. This cabinet wall, sixteen inches deep and eight feet wide, incorporates compartments for pots and pans, upper cupboards for less frequently used utensils, and a china cupboard. The cupboards as well as the cutlery drawers can be opened from either the dining room or kitchen.

300 Stove and sink, linked by a working surface, are the focal point of this kitchen. All three units are topped with stainless steel. The window arrangement is less satisfactory, for casement windows should be several inches above the working surfaces so as not to interfere with the work beneath. The serving hatch to the dining room has a swinging door on the side with compartments intended for glasses.

298

299

300

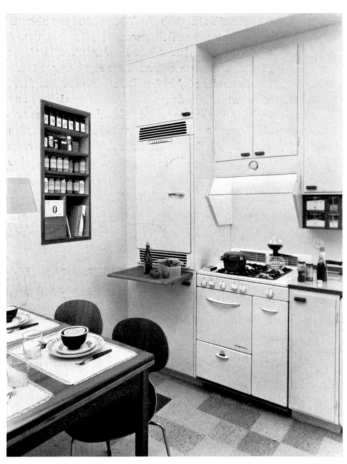

301, 302   The remodeling of this kitchen had to take into account the irregular shape of the room. The architect combined all the different built-in units on one wall, with a refrigerator within easy reach, and a ventilation hood above the stove. Concealed lighting illuminates the working surfaces. A cupboard wall continues into the neighboring utility room for ironing, washing and cleaning. The details are extraordinarily well designed: the teak of the central dining area is repeated in the wall recess, the surrounds of working surfaces and counters, and in the retractable shelf below the refrigerator. The color scheme is not one of strong accents but is aimed at achieving a generally bright effect in the room: whitewashed walls with white or yellow cabinet doors.

301

302

The equipment of this kitchen was chosen to suit the size and shape of the room. For a floor area of over 85 square feet, L-shaped or U-shaped plans are particularly suitable. They ensure an uninterrupted working space with continuous working surfaces along the wall. In rooms which have doors on both short walls (304, 305) this is impossible. The elongated shape (304) leads to two parallel linear arrangements of the individual kitchen units. The kitchen opens into a much-used-workroom; the most important kitchen areas – stove, counter, and sink – along one side so that the housewife need not be disturbed by other members of the family passing through the room. For the kitchen of wider proportions (305) whose second door leads into a little-used room, an interrupted U-shape was chosen.

303

304   This kitchen belongs to a large country house and accordingly had to be equipped with an unusually large battery of refrigerators. The housewife's working surfaces receive daylight from the left. The window is of the right height above the working surfaces.

305   A working kitchen with a hatch on the long wall. A hinged flap, which can be let down, and two stools form the breakfast area.

303   This room next to the kitchen serves for ironing, sewing, and the storage of soiled linen and bulky household utensils, such as ladder, broom, and vacuum cleaner. The work table with its swiveling ironing board is illuminated by a movable wall lamp. The sewing machine is built into a cupboard; the shelves on the left-hand wall are adjustable in height.

304

305

Even in the kitchen, where design is dictated by function, the taste of the owner can still be expressed. The Finnish example (306, 307) has a definite rustic character, with the massive wooden tops of its dining table and counters, and the contrast between timber and white tiles. The American kitchen (308) on the other hand, in which all the units are incorporated in one wall, is distinctly elegant, thanks to the extensive use of mahogany. In one case the kitchen has been treated as a workroom for activities requiring robust and durable furniture; in the other case it has become a streamlined workshop, in which modern technical equipment transforms work into an enjoyable science.

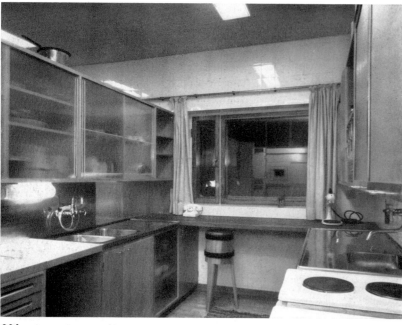

306

307

306, 307   Kitchen and dining area are treated as separate rooms. The main working surface has the best place below the window in this U-shaped arrangement, which has a central cabinet wall to divide the kitchen off from the dining area. The installation of two sinks saves time and labor; the one next to the electric stove is for cleaning vegetables and washing pans, and the other one, below the china cupboard, is for washing dishes. Used china can be put through the hatch on to the draining board and then replaced in the cupboards, whose textured glass doors open to both sides. The sealed parquet floor combines the advantages of a timber floor (warmth and springiness) with imperviousness to water.

308

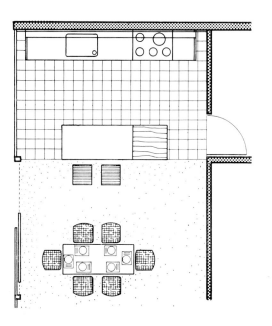

308 In this American house the stove faces a large living room with a dining area. The boarded ceiling runs through both rooms; only the floor tiles distinguish the kitchen and living areas. The working surface and the breakfast bar are sheathed in plastic. The golden-brown timber of the cupboards, together with the extremely neat and tasteful arrangement of the fittings (control panel for the stove and a ventilator for cooking smells) are of great decorative charm and link the cooking wall aesthetically with the rest of the room. The stove and cabinets are laid out in a single row, while the back of the breakfast bar and the adjoining cabinet on the right provide further storage space.

309

310

311

309–314 A desire for flexibility was the decisive consideration in rebuilding this American kitchen. The dining room (313, 314) is shut off from the breakfast area, which is connected with the kitchen by a folding door. The cupboard wall, with doors on either side separating dining room and kitchen, has a beautifully grained walnut surface when closed. When the hatch is open, it affords a view into the kitchen. The sink has been installed within reach of the hatch, while the electric hotplates, broiler, and oven are combined on the opposite side at the correct working height. Part of the terrace was used to house the breakfast bar; the arrangement of the seats by the window was chosen because of the unusually beautiful view. A white plastic blind keeps out the morning sun.

312

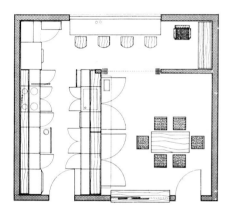

313

314

315

A kitchen completely isolated from the living quarters occupies one end of the scale of possibilities. These solutions show the other extreme: kitchen and living room have become one, and the stove moves into the center of social life. Cooking becomes a family occupation. Both these examples are taken from week-end houses, and it may be presumed that household chores are reduced to the minimum. An essential condition for such a kitchen in the living room must be a good ventilator, which in both these cases constitutes a decorative feature.

315   A large living room with open beam construction. The different zones of the room are marked off by changes of level. The cooking and dining area is a few steps down from the living area. Electric hotplates and a grill have been let into the plastic top of the stove below an enormous ventilation hood. A room-divider with built-in cupboards contains counter, sink, oven, and refrigerator.

316

316   This week-end house is considerably less expensive. The working surface below the windows is well lit, and an open cupboard to the right of the stove houses the most essential utensils. The blue and white tiled stove below the ventilation hood, together with the boarded ceiling, gives a gay country atmosphere to the whole room.

317

318

317, 318   One disadvantage of the working kitchen is its complete isolation from the rest of the house, especially in households with small children. It is difficult for the housewife who spends a large part of the day in the kitchen to supervise her children. Here the problem has been solved by making an adjacent room into a playroom. The actual kitchen area has a very casual plan. Sink and stove are combined in a free-standing kitchen block, which leaves plenty of room to move about and has the additional advantage of accessibility from all sides.

The bedroom

The bedroom

The modern style of living has brought about decisive changes in bedrooms. To begin with, bedroom furniture has become lightweight and practical, and as in other rooms, there is a tendency to stress simplicity and practicality. Complex moldings, carvings in dark woods, and ornate mirrors, have been replaced by smooth surfaces in veneers or strong colors that are easier to maintain. Even plastic laminates and steel tubes for frames are now appropriate for bedroom furnishings. The second change concerns the function of the bedroom. Nowadays it is more and more frequently becoming a multi-purpose room. Its use is no longer restricted to eight or ten night hours; as the quietest room in the house, it now provides a place to which to retire and work undisturbed during the day. The housewife, in particular, can derive benefit from additional use of the bedroom. This is not merely a makeshift arrangement dictated by restrictions of space in a small apartment. In large houses too the bedroom is often expanded by the addition of a desk, bookshelves, and a reading corner. If we look for the real reason, we must consider first the tendency toward the interpenetration of spatial functions and then the preference for living in a large multi-purpose room rather than more private but smaller individual rooms.

How does this change of style affect the individual piece of furniture? Beds have generally become lower in recent years. The heavy bedstead with tall headboards belongs just as much to the past as the little bedside cupboard with its box-like structure and marble top and the wash stand with flowered china wash basin and jug. Now divans without headboards and with mattresses resting on low frames are the order of the day. In place of the bedside cupboard there is a simple table or shelf, with drawers or hinged flaps suspended from it. Since it has become possible to buy commercially produced wall cabinets which can be made up according to individual needs from standard units, the wall cabinet has gradually replaced the free-standing wardrobe. Reaching right up to the ceiling, these have top compartments to provide additional storage space. Thus, in the bedroom too, furnishing means buying single items rather than a 'suite'.

319

319 An intimate bedroom which proves that generous elegance can be achieved by modern means, when proportions, choice of materials, and color scheme harmonize as well as they do in this example in a New York apartment.

320

321

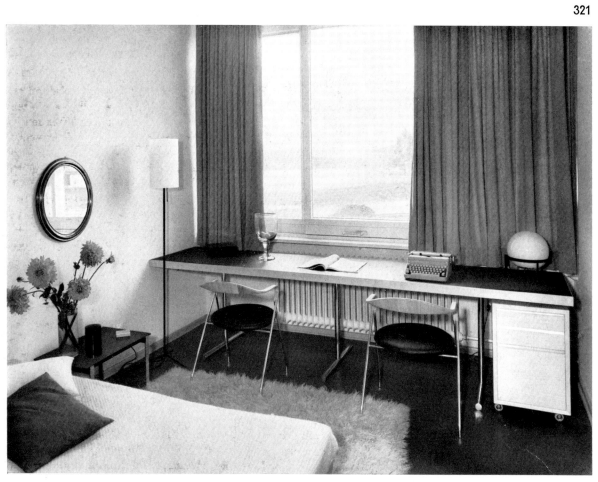

322

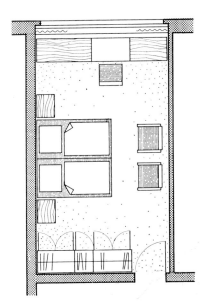

320-322 In modern apartments, the bedroom is frequently planned on these lines: the room is entered from a door in the short wall, which often contains built-in closets. The window in the opposite wall frequently extends the entire width of the room. Next to the door we find the wardrobe, preferably built-in. If – as is usual in a double room – the beds are to be placed side by side, the room plan permits only one solution, namely, to push their headboards against a long wall with the beds projecting at right angles into the room. Very often there is only a narrow passage between the foot of the bed and the other long wall, so that the chest of drawers has to be placed near the window. As it has gradually become more usual to provide some kind of desk or table in the bedroom, the alignment of drawer and table elements beneath the window has become the most practical solution.

We illustrate three examples of this standard type. They demonstrate a number of other common traits that characterize the modern bedroom. Pillows and quilts disappear into a cupboard during the day wherever possible. A smooth cover is spread over the bedding, and where the mattresses themselves have a suitable cover material, even the bedding is removed. Thus beds begin to look more like couches, which underlines the living-room character that the bedroom acquires from serving as a working area for the housewife. Curtains often extend the whole width of the room even when the window is narrower. When the curtain is drawn, one unified area is thereby created along the window wall. The curtains nearly always run on rails fixed close up to the ceiling. The bedside cupboards once in vogue have become low tables or light shelves.

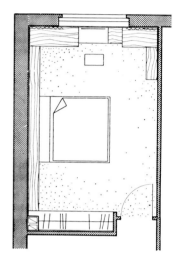

323

323–326   The standard plan has here been ingeniously elaborated to produce a solution with many little 'extras'. In the recess beside the door, a closet with four doors has been built in. The compartment for bed linen is illuminated by concealed strip lighting, which switches on automatically when the door is opened. Along the wall behind the double bed runs a low box unit; the top can be lifted in the center section and at left inclined at various angles. Inside it is painted white to reflect a built-in strip light. At each side of the bed, fitted units with drop fronts serve as bedside tables. Curtains cover the walls on either side of the window to create the impression that it extends from wall to wall. Strip lighting behind the curtain rail gives the effect of daylight. The light behind the translucent glass of the dressing table is switched on when the cosmetic drawer below the glass top is opened.

324

325

326

327

323   The restrained color scheme of the French bedroom illustrated on the opposite page is based upon the vividly grained lemonwood veneer, which is used horizontally for the long drawer unit and vertically on the wardrobe. Here and there dark red rosewood has been used for contrast. The floor is covered with a fitted carpet in red shaded to ochre. The wallpaper has a calligraphic pattern in white on gray, with the colors reversed on the opposite wall. The bedspread and bedframe cover are of raw silk. The curtains feature stripes in quiet shades of gray, green, blue, and yellow.

327   The warm coloring of this simply furnished Swedish bedroom comes from the harmonious combination of the two kinds of wood principally employed: the yellow birch of the short wall and the reddish pine of the boarded ceiling and wall, together with the similar shade of red of the pearwood shelf and dressing table. The strongest color accent is provided by the dark blue and black striped woolen covers on the twin beds.

328

328 A large-scale bedroom scheme with a heavy double bed as the focal point. The frame, on which the mattress rests, is covered with the same checkered material as the bedspread and pillow cases. The headboard, a continuous screen of wooden slats, supports shelves clipped onto it at various heights. Immediately above the bed the slats are lightly upholstered with a cloth cover. A group of switches next to the bed controls the various sources of illumination: wall lamps, table lamp, standard lamp for general room lighting. The sitting group in the corner contrasts the curved shapes of the nineteenth-century easy chairs with the square glass-topped table and its tubular steel frame.

329

329   Although this Italian bedroom has been furnished with economical
means, its size and the valuable antiques it features give it an air of luxury.
The inlaid chest in the foreground, the Baroque candlestick, the carpet,
wooden sculpture, and painting are all deliberately chosen pieces which
form a subtle contrast to the otherwise severe room. The calm atmosphere
of the room is not without an element of tension: the heavy woolen bed
cover, for example, set against the smooth marble floor, the consciously
chosen asymmetrical placing of the picture, and the elongation of the bed
headboard to the right. On the left of the bed is a large shelf with a suspended compartment for magazines. The lamps are adjustable and have cylindrical
metal reflectors.

330

331

332

333

330, 331   A successful combination of modern and antique furniture: tubular steel chairs, suspended drawer units, and an old secretary desk with matching armchair.

332   This Swedish bedroom has also old furniture and is arranged on the standard plan (322). The Biedermeier accent of bureau and chair is continued in the other furnishings: in the pastel pictures, the white curtains, and the color combination of the striped bedspread.

333   In contrast to the colored illustration above, this is a cool and distinguished scheme made up of cubes and planes. The wall shelf at the head of the bed incorporates concealed lighting. A section can be raised to serve as a pillow support.

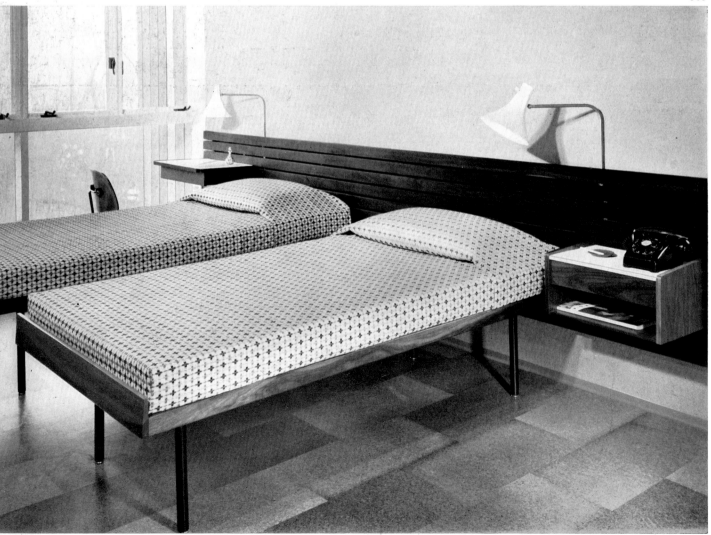

334

334-337 Two bedrooms with separate beds. One case (334, 335) is a sensible, practical solution that hardly differs from the normal double-bed arrangement. The second bedroom, however (336, 337), differs considerably from the usual, both in arrangement and type of furniture. In a room of irregular plan, the beds stand far apart and face in opposite directions. Their simple metal frames form a subtle contrast to the rich antique chest of drawers and the Baroque painting above it. A few playful details, like the putto on the wall, the glass ball below the ceiling beam, or the oval frame of mirror and picture, mitigate the room's ascetic severity. In the economy of effects, much taste can be discerned in the way that antique and modern elements have been harmonized.

334, 335 The beds, though moved apart, have been joined visually by the long slatted headboard. Bedside units of various types can be hooked into the spaces between the slats. The floor consists of cork tiles in different shades.

335

336

337

336, 337 An Italian bedroom with white-washed walls and a polished marble floor. Beds in mat-black tubular steel with gleaming brass caps on bedposts and feet. Adjustable bed lamps with black cylindrical metal shades. White linen curtains. Chairs and doors upholstered with the same material as the bedspreads.

338

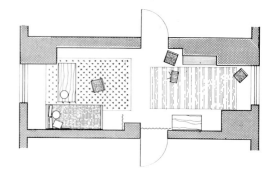

339

340

338-341 A charming section: the attic bedroom. When it comes to the romantic, the young French girl who lives in the attic of a venerable old house in Saint-Germain-des Prés wins hands down (338, 339). After all, three centuries contributed to the furnishing of her angular room. An attic can also assume a very personal character with contemporary elements, as is shown by an American example (340), whose broad expanse of painted wooden walls, graphically accentuated by joists, provides the background for the arrestingly placed picture and the constant play of the Calder mobile. In the attic of their house (341) a Swedish couple have made themselves a sleeping alcove by the simplest means. Incidentally, this example proves how light and spacious an attic can appear despite its sloping walls if the roof timbers are left exposed.

338, 339 This small angular attic room has a timeless quality with its old walnut furniture (chairs, chest of drawers, antique desk and bed) to which the few modern pieces (blue and white striped curtains, carpets, plastic-covered wire bookshelves, table lamp with bottle base) have been added. The long narrow room can be divided by a curtain.

341

340 The boarded walls and the roof panels
between the rafters have been left bare in
parts, while other parts have been painted.
Similarly, the choice of the remaining materials is very varied: the pillow covers and
bedspread are made of leather, the floor is
of stone slabs, and in front of the bed – as a
contrast to the rather harsh atmosphere – a
shaggy fur rug has been spread.

341 The close boarding of the stair well,
stained a vivid brown, also forms the side of
the bed recess which, like the triangular
gable wall, is papered with a blue striped
pattern that stresses the height of the room.
The ceiling surfaces between the beams are
painted white, the floor boards pinkish-gray.
The frill at the cross bar of the alcove, the
white curtains and bedspreads emphasize the
pleasant and comfortable atmosphere.

342

342   A wide clothes and linen cupboard has been inserted into the alcove next to the bathroom, whose door is faced with a tall mirror. As space was limited, sliding doors were used. If necessary, an upper compartment can be added.

These four variations on the installation of a closet in a bedroom show attempts to keep a large floor area free and at the same time provide maximum storage space for clothes and linen. All have one thing in common, letting the wardrobe disappear into the wall: in Fig. 342 by pushing a normal wardrobe into an alcove; in Fig. 343 by turning an alcove into a walk-in closet; in the top example on the right, by building a closet into the window wall.

344   The closet wall by the window consists of two three-part elements. Behind the three doors there is room on the left for coats and dresses, on the right for jackets and shoes, and in the middle there are drawers and shelves for underwear, hats, and bags. Concealed lighting above the window illuminates that part of the room. The headboard of the bed contains radio, telephone, and built-in compartments with plastic-lined drop doors to serve as bedside tables. The cylindrical lamps with metal half shades can be turned to give direct or indirect light. All wooden parts are walnut; the floor and window platform are fitted with blue pile carpets. The walls are white, the ceiling black, and the bedspreads mustard yellow; the easy chair has black leather covers and a walnut frame.

343

343   If a recess next to the bedroom is deep enough, it can be made into a walk-in closet. In this example, the recess was closed in by room-high pine boarding. It can be entered by an ordinary door and has a rod for hanging clothes on the left and a chest of drawers on the right.

344

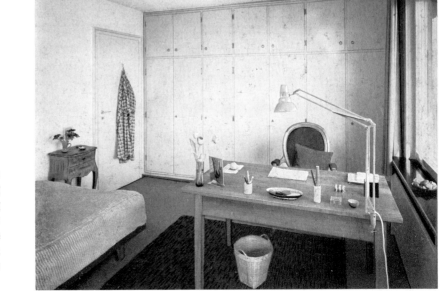

345

345   In a comparatively small room, which has hardly enough space for free-standing cabinets, a closet wall has been built along the entire end. In this way the maximum floor area was kept free and plenty of storage space made available. The off-white paint makes the wall appear to recede and gives the room a more spacious appearance.

346

347

346, 347   One side of this bedroom is completely masked by a wooden wall into which has been built a five-part wardrobe with corresponding upper compartments. A long shelf with two drawer units runs beneath the window. As the room is comparatively low, a light, perpendicularly striped veneer was used on the wardrobe wall which, like the striped curtains, emphasizes the vertical.

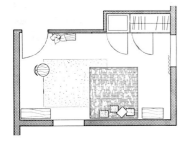

348, 349   Here the situation was the reverse of the previous example. The relatively small room is too high. To counteract this visually, stress was laid on the horizontal – by the wall treatment behind the bed and the division of the built-in fittings. The lemonwood front of the clothes cupboard is drawn out in width; the gray door of the linen compartment has a gray rectangular wall strip beside it, while the white drawer fronts and the adjoining wall surface together make up a light horizontal band. The Venetian blind with its plastic blades conceals a door to a terrace.

348

349

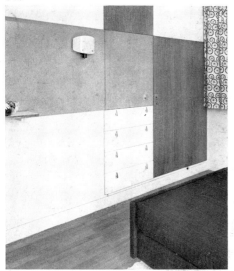

350–352 To create the optical illusion that this small, almost square room is wider on one side than on the other, a five-foot-wide teak sliding door opens into the living room (351 right). The same timber is used for the boarding behind the double bed, whose frame is covered with red cloth. The geometric pattern of the functional division of the built-in closet opposite the foot of the bed, is stressed by the teak strips that edge the doors. The sliding doors of the clothes cabinet are painted white and have leather loops as handles. The blue hinged door on the right has a tall mirror on its inside face; it shuts on a compartment with interchangeable drawers. The upper shelves are made of glass for better visibility. The doors of the two compartments below the ceiling are practical because they are top-hinged and can be pushed up.

350

351

352

On these pages the interplay of textures dominates the decor. Natural materials like teak and oiled rosewood contrast with man-made surfaces of glass, steel, and brightly painted walls and doors. Rugs of deep blue wool act as a foil to the display of textures, while at the same time differentiating the two areas of bed and dressing table.

353

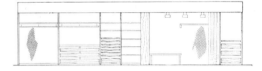

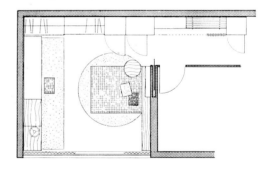

354

353–357   A comparatively small bedroom with a calm and cozy air, which it derives from carefully chosen materials and warm colors. By stressing the horizontal it is made to look wider than it really is. The wall opposite the large window in this almost square room has been turned into a closet which continues into the anteroom (353, 354). An accordion-type folding door conceals a bench and a series of shelves with sliding coat hooks, and a sliding door divides the dressing room from the actual bedroom. The closet front alternates panels of rosewood with-red-and-white sliding doors. The chest units at the head of the double bed store bedding in the daytime and hold a radio and telephone (356). A little to one side are glass bookshelves and a wooden newspaper rack. Above the headboard a strip light with white metal front provides a reading light, and next to the bed stands a pivoting circular table of adjustable height. On the opposite wall are placed a dressing table and desk with a glass top (357).

355

356

357

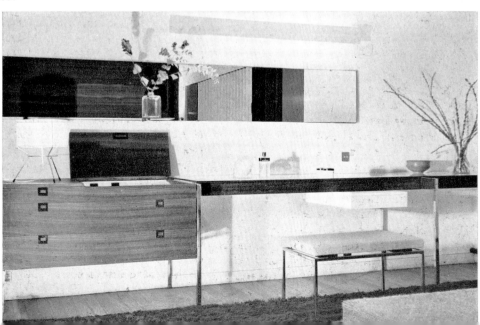

358

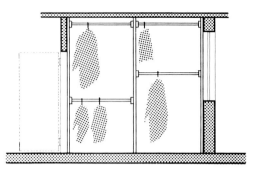

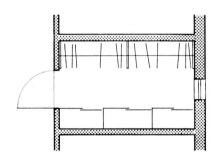

358   A walk-in closet with four coat rods on one side, and open shelves and sliding door compartments on the other. Drawers accommodate small items such as handkerchiefs and stockings. Shoes and suitcases can be stored below. The light is fixed above the coat rails.

358-360   The walk-in closet is ideal to store clothes and underwear. Where a built-in closet wall would occupy too much floor space or take up valuable wall space against which furniture and shelves could be placed, the walk-in closet often requires only the width of an ordinary and unobtrusive door, leaving the remaining wall area available for other uses. The internal fittings may be designed to individual needs, and with skillful subdivision, the capacity can be surprisingly large. One side is nearly always fitted with one or more rods from which to hang dresses, coats, skirts, and jackets. The example above shows a very practical rod set low for children's clothes, which the child can reach easily.

The other side has open compartments for hats, sweaters, and bed and table linen, with low shelves for shoes and closed drawers to protect shirts or underwear from dust. There is nearly always sufficient room in the walk-in closet to store winter or summer clothing instead of packing it away in mothballs and dust covers. Fig. 360 shows how a walk-in closet can be added, combined with a sleeping alcove of the same depth.

359   This walk-in closet is built into a young girl's room. On the left (visible in the door mirror) there are open shelves for sweaters, underwear, and shoes. On the right, below the clothes, is room for bedding behind a grille of vertical timber slats. Over the door are further storage compartments with sliding doors accessible from the room.

359

360

360   A combination of walk-in closet and sleeping alcove. In contrast to the other two examples, the coat rod here runs across the closet, to cope with its shallow depth. On the left is a series of adjustable shelves.

361

361-363   The comparison of these two solutions is not to show the differences in detailing but to point out the main contrasts in the over-all conception of the rooms. It might be said that a modification of the architectural setting, which is the issue here, is only possible when one builds one's own home. But these two examples, although each one is different, demonstrate something of general value, that it is possible to re-create their atmospheres with certain changes and limitations in more conventional houses. Two different ideas confront each other here: the conception of the bedroom as a place of refuge which shuts off the outside world, and the idea, on the other hand, of an open room in close contact with its surroundings, the garden, and the landscape, where the barrier between inside and outside disappears.

361   A room which emphasizes the impression of safety, evoked by the unbroken wall areas and the slanting ceiling and underlined again by the close boarding. Its warm tone dominates the room in which the broken white of the closely woven curtain affords a diffused light during the day. The artificial lighting is adapted to this soft coloring and mood: the hanging lamp which gives a mellow light, and the spot lamp which shines on the curtain for general illumination.

362, 363   In contrast to Fig. 361, this is an open room, in which solid walls have been reduced to a minimum. The sliding glass walls (362) give the illusion of living in the open. As the house is screened by trees, curtains could be dispensed with. The transparency of the room's confines is continued even on the inside. A wall screen like a Japanese sliding door is framed above the double bed; its square panels allow enough light to filter through to the dressing table and two bureaus which separate the dressing room behind the screen from the bedroom proper. The backs of these chests form the headboard of the bed. The impression of transparency and lightness is also reinforced by the furniture, which is supported on slender white enameled steel tubes.

362

363

364

364-366   Two examples from a multitude of possibilities that group the bed-room and its supplementary accommodations, such as bathroom and dress-ing room, into an organic whole that might be termed a 'functional cell'. This carefully planned room-sequence forms its own center of gravity inside the house. In each case closet doors run along the long wall, tending to stress the room's length. As can be clearly seen from our two examples, the beds have also been placed to conform with this longitudinal stress.

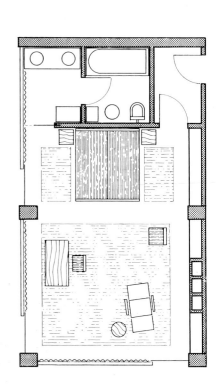

364   As the plan shows, the rooms adjoining the bedroom lie beyond the narrow wall behind the bed. The door on the right leads into an anteroom, which links the bedroom with the rest of the house; the doorway on the left opens into the dressing room and the bathroom. A row of closets runs along the right-hand wall. Brick-faced piers provide visual separation be-tween the bedroom area and the living area in the foreground, and antique furnishings emphasize the luxurious character of the whole room.

365, 366   In this bedroom, the double bed has been placed as a free-standing unit in the center of the room. At its head stands a double-side cabinet, which can be used as a night table. It has compartments for bedding in front and bureau drawers at the back. Lighting fixtures built into the low translucent screen provide illumination for reading and dressing. The area behind the cabinet serves as a dressing room. The window wall, with a large sliding door leading on to a terrace, is almost entirely of glass. The opposite wall consists of room-high cabinets with sliding doors of laminated plastic. Three mahogany doors punctuate the end wall: the one at the left leads to the vestibule, the center door to the bathroom, and the one at the right to a shower. A mirror extending from floor to ceiling is helpful for dressing and also makes the room look larger.

365

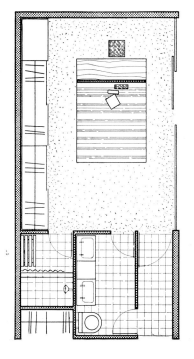

366

367

367 The projection of the bathroom and closet wall into the bedroom here creates two alcoves, each of which has been fitted with a dressing table. The closet with sliding doors between two whitewashed wall slabs holds dresses and coats on the left and blouses on the right. The small drawer unit below is for underwear. Lights concealed by the glass panels above the closet provide soft indirect illumination. The color scheme draws its effect from the warm tones of the boarded ceiling and the different colors of the painted walls.

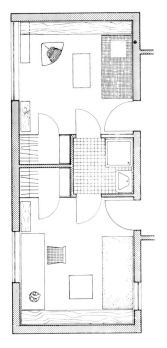

368

368   While in the preceding examples (364–366) the bathroom and dressing
room have been grouped in one unit along the narrow wall of the bedroom,
in this example they have been placed between two separate bedrooms.
This suite of rooms has been located in the quietest part of the house. Each
bedroom has its own walk-in closet and door to the common bathroom.
Floor space has been conserved by placing additional storage compartments,
accessible by ladder, below the ceiling.

369

370

369, 370   Two master bedrooms are separated in these examples by cabinet walls that open to either side and contain built-in desks and dressing tables. By incorporating several units into this one storage wall, the owners in each case were able to dispense with additional furniture and thus save floor space. The continuous fitted carpet indicates that the two rooms have been treated as one. Both share a view into the garden through a large window wall. The doors of the two closet walls have been treated quite differently in each case. In the example above, the narrow doors are articulated by old engravings of town views. In the lower picture the contrast of colored panels produces a lively composition of squares and rectangles.

371

Whether a double bed, twin beds, or separate beds are chosen for the parents' bedroom is not just a problem of space and furniture, but above all a question of personal preference. The sleeping habits of the two partners are frequently so different that separate rooms are preferred – provided that sufficient space is available.

371   In this spacious bedroom, which has been divided by both the cabinet wall and the color scheme, the two beds have been placed in opposite corners; the second bed – not visible here – has its head next to the chest of drawers visible on the left of the picture. Desk and easy chairs were readily accommodated in this generously proportioned room. The cork-tiled floor forms a unified warm background with which the strong blues of the wardrobe and bedspread contrast effectively.

372

373

372-376   The unpractical, now neglected dressing table of blessed memory, with its fixed center mirror and two hinged wings, was always rather reminiscent of the triptychs from Gothic altars; it generally dominated some dark corner in solitary state. This monster is disappearing from the modern bedroom, and its place is being taken by the simple cosmetic table. In shape it is either purely functional, consisting of a broad top, suspended drawers, and a well-lit mirror, or else it is in a boudoir style which lends a somewhat playful note to the bedroom.

372   Below the plastic top of this console-shaped dressing table are two drawers. The mirror is so large that it makes the whole room look bigger. On the right is an adjustable louvered window of opaque glass.

374

375

373   This example also features a tall mirror that enlarges the room: the window wall appears wider because of the reflection. The table, which runs on casters, can be extended by leaves on either side and used as a bedside table when pushed up close to the bed. The hanging lamp, visible on the left, runs along a grooved rail in the ceiling, so that it is adjustable not only in height but can also be moved sideways.

374   A simple wooden ledge serves as both dressing and bedside table. An old mirror in a lyre-shaped frame produces a striking effect against the pale wall. In the foreground is a table for writing or sewing.

375   Units of Swedish design – two chests of drawers and a table – have been combined with a spherical lamp and a circular mirror suspended before a curtain to make a graceful ensemble.

376

376   In this Swedish bedroom, the sewing and writing desk consists of a simple table top which has been placed on two low chests. The dressing table is also improvised out of a blue enameled wall shelf with a rectangular mirror above.

377

377   A dressing and work table directly below the window has been made from a small chest, a cupboard, and a table with a two-piece, hinged top. The miniature bureau, with its many drawers for jewelry, sewing equipment, and other necessities, is in commercial production in Sweden.

378

The idea that a bedroom is simply for sleeping went out with fancy cushions and high-gloss furniture. More and more frequently the housewife sets aside space in the bedroom for leisure occupations. This practice need not necessarily be restricted to apartment-dwellers cramped for space; it can be a way of giving added character to a bedroom while also providing quiet and privacy for work. This can be accomplished with an air of luxury as in Fig. 378 or with the simplest means, as in the two examples on the left-hand page.

378   The desk in the alcove of this American bedroom is lit by day from a room-high louvered window with adjustable opaque glass blades. The cupboard below the desk is faced in the same light mahogany veneer as the walls. The wall-to-wall woolen carpet matches the natural tones of the wood.

To end this chapter, here are three desks in bedrooms: two made simply, the third (381) more luxurious in color and material. In its own way, each unit offers an imaginative solution to the private work area in the bedroom.

379   A table top has been inserted between a closet and the window wall. A hanging lamp, with a chromium-plated shade and a round mirror, give this writing and sewing corner its pleasant atmosphere.

380   A writing corner has been created here in the minimum of space. The upper drawer of this chest of drawers can be let down for use as a writing surface. With the aid of a mirror it can also be used as an improvised dressing table.

379

380

381

381 This table top and drawer unit have been faced with white plastic, which not only has practical advantages but is the predominant color of the room: on the walls, on the curtains, on the shade of the articulated table lamp. The illustration shows how particularly bright colors have been set against this neutral background.

382

382   A children's room whose arrangement reflects the different ages of the two sisters who share it. In the foreground is the older child's section, the bed at right-angles to the wall, and her desk by the window on the right. In the background is the smaller child's half, with her crib pushed into the corner behind the two standard wardrobes. Against the far wall is a low play table with matching chairs and stools. To the right, at the rear and under the continuous projecting sill, are four toy boxes; farther toward the middle are two suspended drawer units. A gray carpet is fitted over the whole floor. The walls are painted white.

The children's room

The children's room

The nursery or children's room is a house within a house. In one single room many functions are combined that grown-ups usually distribute over at least two rooms: sleeping, eating, living, working (by which is meant any activity at the table from painting and handicrafts to homework), together with the most important: playing. The world of the small child, in which he grows up, forms his ideas, and develops his imagination, is usually contained within the four walls of the nursery, and the limits of his domain should accordingly be extended as far as possible. A tiny room is not suitable, as the child needs a room that gives him as much freedom to move as possible, preferably one on the sunny side of the house, if possible with a balcony or veranda.

If one has a choice of several rooms, or if one decides to build a house, the children's room should be situated in a quiet part. A baby's room should be far from the noise of the living room and near the parents' room.

Nowadays it is generally acknowledged that the child should if possible have a room of his own. The play corner in the living room and the cot in the parents' bedroom can be tolerated only temporarily as emergency arrangements.

We mentioned before that the ideal nursery should give space for freedom of movement: sufficient floor space for a baby to crawl about and for a bigger child to play in. As the following pictures illustrate, there are many ways of saving floor space, even when the rooms are not very big. They all start with the idea of clearing bulky furniture out of the way. Thus, if two children have to share one small room, double-decker bunks provide a suitable solution. The table in the middle of the room can be replaced by a built-in table top, fixed below the window or to a wall. Instead of cupboards and chests of drawers with their corners projecting into the room, a cabinet wall of shallow depth may be used. The furniture industry now makes a number of sectional wall units which can be easily taken apart and rearranged. If this type of cabinet costs more, its usefulness makes up for the extra expense.

Where circumstances permit, the children's room may be supplemented by a special playroom. This division is an advantage, particularly when two or more children grow up together. The ideal solution is a really large separate area for the children; often an attic or basement can be used as a playroom. With this type of arrangement, the size of the nursery is no longer so important.

The teenager, too, may be able to manage with a smaller room. But his new interests require new space: a reading corner should be provided with book case and record player within easy reach. Every hobby requires storage space for sports equipment, musical instruments, or collector's cabinets.

If the question arises as to whether two older children would prefer to share a larger room or live alone in two smaller rooms, they will nearly always choose individual rooms. This need for privacy grows as the child grows up. If only one room is available, some way should be found of making two smaller ones, by means of a solid partition, or at least by visuals eparation with a curtain, a low wall, or a cupboard as a room-divider.

So much for the size and arrangement of the children's room. As regards furnishings we cannot give any hard and fast rules, but the following pages illustrate a number of basic principles which are valid everywhere. One should make an effort to avoid the white-enamel type of nursery, with its hygienic atmosphere, prevalent thirty or forty years ago. Garishness is not appropriate either. Whether a children's room is suitably furnished depends not only on the choice of furniture but also on the wealth of ideas and understanding with which the parents create an atmosphere. A modest but imaginative solution using furniture from the attic can be as cheerful and comfortable as an arrangement which uses the most luxurious equipment. One should not visualize the nursery purely from the aesthetic and rational viewpoint of the grown-up. One must understand the delight a child can take in a wall covered with his own paintings and the magic of furniture that can be pushed around to build houses and castles in the playroom.

Furniture should be of a solid and simple style without complicated me-chanics. Shelves should be within easy reach; drawers and toy boxes should be simple to move; tables should be of the right height and light enough for the child to move about. Certain items are particularly adaptable, such as wooden planks and cubes of different sizes that can be used as stools, tables, or boxes. These materials can be used both as furniture and as building units for the play of the child's own imagination.

The recent idea of buying nursery furniture which can be used later by older children seems at first sight to be a sensible one. But it is doubtful whether baby furniture can possibly be adapted for a teenager. Wear and tear is particularly great in the nursery and can be seen after a few years in spite of polyester paint and plastic surfaces. This reservation apart, adaptability can best be interpreted by a change of purpose, e.g., the toy cupboard can later be used as a bookcase, and shelves that stood on the floor for easy access can be put on a base.

One more word about color in the nursery. Of course there should be color – light gay color. But beware of areas too large and too bright on floor and walls. Colors need to stand out against a neutral background so that they don't cancel each other. Walls are best left white. This may sound impractical at first, but there are many washable paints that are quite suitable for the nursery. Those who prefer wallpaper should choose a neutral one with a small pattern and a light background. While the children are small, the floor should be carpeted. Bigger children need a smooth floor, preferably of linoleum or plastic tiles. Once there is a neutral background, one can introduce color: on the cupboard doors, on the curtains, bedspreads, and cushions. In addition to all this there will be the little splashes of color from toys, books, or the child's own drawings.

For the rest, a color scheme in the nursery is largely a matter of personal taste. The primary colors red, yellow, and blue are often preferred, but pastel shades can be just as suitable. So many color combinations depend on fashion influences that change from year to year that one should not attempt to make rules.

This small child's room has been equipped with simple furniture correctly proportioned for a child, with cupboard units that can later be extended by the purchase of additional items.

383

384

385

386

When furnishing a nursery, the best arrangement is one which allows even a small child the maximum freedom of movement. Where no built-in cabinets are available, it is best to group free-standing chests and cupboards in such a way that a large play area is formed in the rest of the room. A large carpet provides a suitable space for the explorations of a child learning to crawl and walk. Apart from the growing bed, and the crib with railings adjustable to different heights, the furniture industry also offers various types of 'growing' beds, which can be transformed from a baby's bed to a teenager's divan. It may be readily imagined that the principle of furniture that 'grows with the child' could be applied to all the equipment needed for a nursery, perhaps with the aid of unit furniture or interchangeable built-in units, which are gradually added to the original fittings. In practice, however, this solution will generally miscarry, because nursery furniture is subjected to particularly hard wear and becomes shabby after a few years. Besides, the blocks, boxes, and planks that a child needs for his creative play can no longer be used by older children.

387

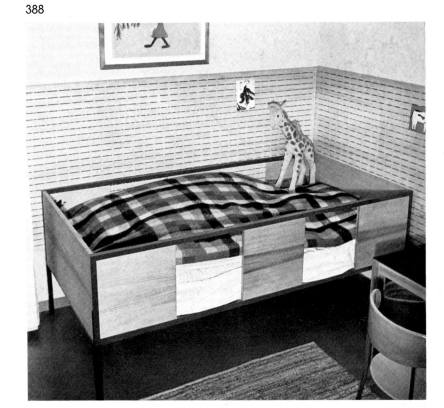

388

384-386   The railings of the 'growing bed' can be taken off and used as a playpen. The curtained-off cupboard for baby things at the foot of the bed can later be used for toy shelves and a bedside table. Fig. 384 shows three toy boxes that slip inside one an other with a top board whose dowels fit into the rows of holes.

387   A nursery in an attic, with good use, made of the way the room is laid out. The sloping corner was used for a built-in wall cupboard. The crib with its let-down railings has been put on the chest of drawers to save space. The play area on the floor has been supplemented by the upholstered window seat. (The window itself has been made safe with special fittings).

388   The alternation of solid and void squares dispels any feeling of boxy heaviness in this cot made of rectangular steel tubes and cherrywood. The lattice at the back serves as a wall-guard and bulletin board.

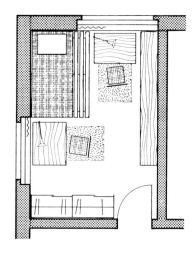

389

389   Corner room with a two-tier bunk in the angle between the windows. A handy bench is firmly anchored to the lower bed and serves as a ledge for dressing, as a night table, and as a step. A steel rung on the bed post (here next to the window) makes climbing into the upper bunk easier. The adjustable table lamp also serves as a bed light. In front of each window is a single desk (see plan). Next to the door is a built-in closet with sliding doors.

390

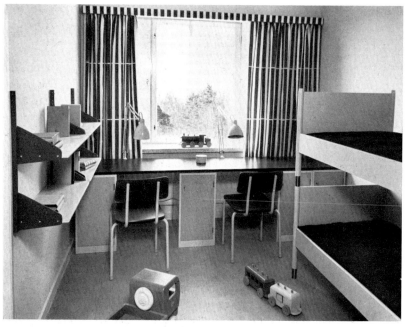

390   A room for two with a double-decker bunk and well-built double desk by the window. The table top reaches from wall to wall and rests on four identical cupboards with colored doors.

391

391 In this nursery, the double-decker bunks, one of which projects beyond the other, are made of the cheapest materials; the sides of the beds are of chipboard, and the toy boxes, painted on the outside only, are of pine. The simple bench running along the wall between bed and window has numerous uses. A quieter pattern for wallpaper and curtains (here of the same design) might have been more suitable in this already colorful room.

389-398 When two children have to share a small room, a double-decker bunk is a solution which nearly always has the enthusiastic approval of the children. Although the upper beds generally have a protective railing (389, 391), it is advisable to put the smaller child in the lower bunk, for then he will not need help to get in and out of bed. It is, of course, essential to allow enough space between the beds so that the child in the lower bunk can sit up comfortably. There is more room for movement when the beds are staggered slightly in relation to each other (391); in such cases the additional space can be utilized by building in play chests or drawers.

The use of a double-decker bunk is particularly suitable for school-children who require two well-lit desks near the window in a comparatively long and narrow room, as well as enough space for dressing and recreation. If, for example, the upper bed in Fig. 390 were to be moved over to the left-hand wall, only a very narrow passage would remain between the beds. If, as in Fig. 389, a corner room is available with windows on two different walls, single desks can be installed below each window. Fig. 391 shows a slightly larger room with a continuous desk top along the window wall at the right.

392

392   Of the following four examples of bedrooms with double-decker bunks, this room in a Swedish holiday housé shows the most romantic solution with the simplest means. The two beds are fixed in a wood-lined alcove. A chain with a curtain hanging from it acts as a guard rail for the upper bunk. It can be unhooked for making the bed.

393   Here the upper bed is suspended from the ceiling by a steel cable. The color scheme is determined by the timber ceiling, bed frame, and cork-tile floor. Below the lower bed are two drawers. Curtains and lamp-shade are of the same material.

394   An L-shaped corner arrangement which does not hamper the freedom of movement of the child in the lower bed in any way. The upper bed rests on a cross rail at the wall and on chromium-plated steel tubes at the other end.

395   Two bunks, one projecting beyond the other, with wooden frames. Footholds have been cut into one of the boards to act as a ladder. Storage space is curtained off below the upper bed.

393

394

395

In rooms for more than two children space-saving arrangement[s] for beds are particularly important. After all, this room mu[st] provide enough cupboard and closet space for three or fo[ur] children as well as a large play area. When it is not possible [to] provide separate sleeping quarters for this number of childre[n] much planning is required to design a room to contain the thr[ee] main functions of sleeping, playing, and working.

Fig. 407 indicates how this can be achieved: light partition wa[lls] separate the bed cubicles from the room and also accommoda[te] separate small desks. Thus each child has his own small doma[in] into which he can retire, while the remaining area serves as [a] playroom for all. The same basic principle of creating a priva[te] zone for each child can be achieved by half-height chests [of] drawers between the beds in Fig. 406. In this way, cubicles ha[ve] been made in an otherwise undivided room.

Where the shape or size of the room does not allow this ki[nd] of division, or where, as in the examples on the right, thr[ee] children of almost the same age want to share one large roo[m,] the question of how to create space assumes special signi[fi-] cance. One space-saver is to combine cupboards and drawe[rs] into one built-in storage wall.

The main problem, however, is to find a space-saving solutio[n] for the beds. The pictures on these two pages demonstrate tw[o] possibilities: a group of two double-decker bunks and thr[ee] single beds of different heights on casters that can be stack[ed] against the wall during the day.

396   The pair of double-decker bunks in this example ha[s] been partitioned off from the rest of the room by a wall of sla[ts.] The rear wall and the ceiling are lined with unpainted boar[ds.] The foot of each bed is supported by the railings. Beds, railin[gs,] and ceiling bars are painted white, while the red partition pr[o-] vides the main color accent, and the pastel bedcovers blend [in] harmoniously.

396

7

398

7, 398   A large nursery in an American house. The three
bular steel beds stack one below the other. Along one wall,
neath a row of high-level windows, are suspended cupboards
th sliding doors, and below them runs a continuous table top.
movable toy chest forms part of each desk. There is direct
cess to a walled-in yard which serves as an extension of the
ay area. The colors are restricted to pastel tones of yellow,
een, and blue, and each child has his own color repeated on
dcover, work table, cupboard, and bureau. Color accents:
rk gray beams, and brilliant red tractor seats on metal legs.

399

400

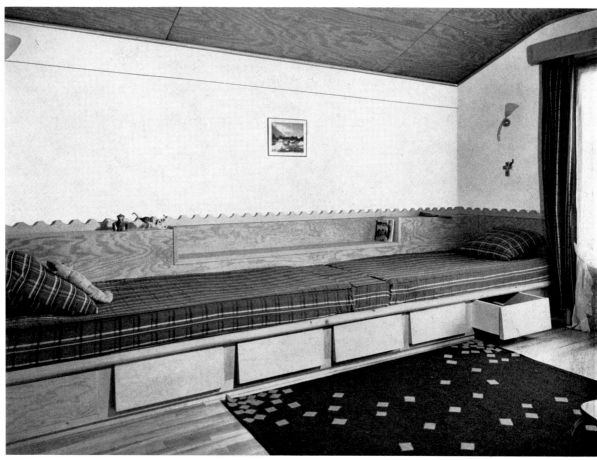

401

399-402 Four examples of double rooms with the beds along one wall. Single beds have the advantages over double-decker bunks of adaptability, durability (the children cannot use them as jungle gyms), and accessibility. The beds can also be used as seats in the daytime, and even as an additional play area. For narrow rooms (400, 402) there are certain disadvantages: placing the beds in one long row gives the room the appearance of a passage, and there is no opportunity of putting two desks below the window.

402

399 Large gable room furnished as bedroom and playroom for two children. The two beds along the wall are separated by a chest of drawers. The glass wall, ventilated by two sash windows, allows light to flood the room. A long, low play table stands before the window. The large expanse of plastic-tiled floor gives ample space for the children to play.

400 Double room with beds and desks parallel to the long walls. Two hanging lamps with non-glare metal shades illuminate the desk and supplement the insufficient daylight from the window. Further storage is provided on adjustable wall shelves.

401 The two beds on the long wall of this nursery make a continuous seat for daytime use. In the center of the rear wall is a built-in bookshelf, and there are drawers in the base of the beds. Ceiling, molding, and bed are covered with the same light veneer.

402 Scheme for a small room with the divans against the wall. This arrangement, however, leaves space for only one desk.

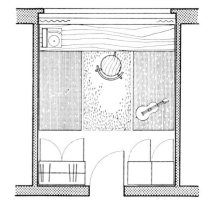

403

404

403 Smallest scheme, with one divan against each of the long walls. Here the room of a young jazz fan has been furnished with a desk top stretching from wall to wall. The second divan provides seating for visiting friends. The door is flanked by built-in closets.

404 An L-shaped arrangement of divans in a Swedish room for a young girl. This makes good use of available space and looks comfortable. Color scheme in pastel tones: light blue, medium blue, turquoise, and a contrasting pink wall.

405

405 An L-shaped divan arrangement in front of a wall painted in contrasting colors. A tall shelf unit serves as a room-divider between the sleeping area and the rest of the room.

406

406 An American room for three girls. As the windows are set high, it was possible to place two divan beds along that wall. Chests of drawers, the higher one with a bookshelf in the side, divide the room visually. The other long wall has been completely fitted with cabinets. Each girl has her own alcove in a different color, with drawers and a rail for blouses and jackets, as well as an adjoining closet with a sliding door which can be locked. The central heating operates through grilles in the floor and not through radiators, which made it possible to place the beds below the window. This solution provides ample storage and floor space.

407   In a larger room of approximately 13 by 15 feet with suitably spaced windows, two bed cubicles with well-lit desks have been partitioned off. In order not to clutter the remaining play area with individual pieces of furniture, a continuous cupboard wall was built-in next to the door.

407

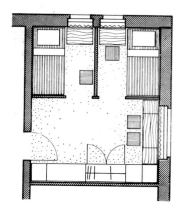

The illustrations and plans on these two pages show examples which may be considered ideal for the accommodation of two or three older children. Separate bedrooms are connected by the common playroom, so that each child can play with his brothers and sisters or read and work undisturbed in the quiet of his own room.

This type of arrangement does not necessarily require whole suites as illustrated in Figs. 408 and 409; it can also be achieved on a smaller scale by inserting partitions in a large room to create separate sleeping cubicles. Fig. 407 is a good example of this.

Figs. 410 and 411 illustrate an interesting variation which can serve as an inspiration when redesigning one's own house: the basement was made into a playroom with a folding partition that allows the bedroom to open into the play area during the day. Ideally, playrooms should have acoustic-tile ceilings to deaden the noise. The floor should be covered with linoleum or plastic or cork tiles.

408

408   Here, three sons have their own domain, away from the living room and sleeping quarters of their parents. Both bedrooms (the smaller one for the eldest, the larger for the two younger ones who sleep in double-decker bunks) open into the playroom. There are adjustable shelves in the playroom recesses; a bulletin board hangs on the left. The ceiling is covered with perforated acoustic tiles and the floor with plastic tiles.

409 Special attention has been paid to deadening the sound from this playroom, which has two adjoining bedrooms. The ceiling is of acoustic tiles and the floor has a warm, springy, cork surface. The walls are also of cork, with a panel cut out for a blackboard. The color scheme, however, is rather restless with its many different-colored areas and busy-patterned curtains.

409

410, 411 The two bed settees are placed one above the other in the daytime in order to allow the bedroom, which can be partitioned off by a folding wall, to supplement the play area. The two cabinets on the right have washable sides on which the children can paint and draw. One wall cabinet is set on casters and can be opened out; a hinged table top is attached to it on one side.

410

411

412

413

412-415 An ingenious Italian scheme, an apparently improvised mixture of simplicity and deliberately chosen accents, where the bedrooms have been extended by a play-room and a large play terrace on a lower floor. The bedroom-workrooms illustrated are a smaller room for two sisters and a long room for three brothers. The boys' room may be divided by a sliding partition, so that the eldest has one half to himself, while the two younger boys share the other half and sleep in double-decker bunks. As a rule, however, the whole room is shared by all of them, especially the sports equipment (climbing frame and punch ball). The exciting color scheme contrasts the light pink, yellow, and gray walls with the strong blue of the plastic floor tiles and the warm reddish tones of the wooden furniture.

412 The beds in the girls' room can be turned into divans in the daytime. At the head of the beds are adjustable lamps. Small shelves can be suspended from the slatted grilles.

413 View toward the other wall in the girls' room. Their long desk top is in front of the large window. On the short wall are two photographic enlargements of sketches by Degas. Ballet bar and red painted bookcase provide the color accents. On the right is a built-in closet with doors of pink laminated plastic.

414 The boys' room. On the right, the single bed of the eldest; to the left, in the background, the double-decker bunk, and next to it the climbing frame which also serves as a ladder to the upper bed.

415 A desk top spanning the room. Below it are individual tables on casters, which can be pulled out. The shelves at right angles leave the working surface free; the upper shelves can be reached by ladder.

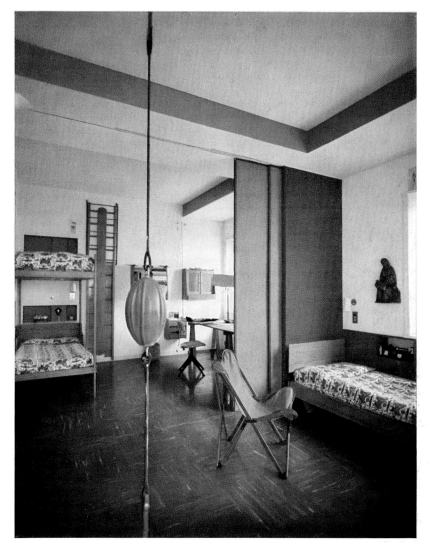
414

415

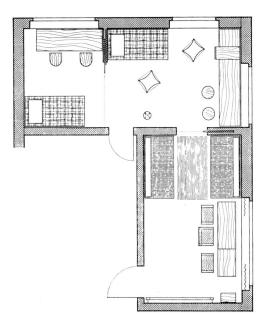

416

416-418 Three children's rooms with a small area where a comfortable atmosphere has been created despite small dimensions. Movable furniture in tiny rooms should obviously be restricted to the minimum and should not be the main feature (as has been shown clearly in Figs. 412–415). It is most important to work out schemes for saving space in small rooms by means of built-in furniture (416) and a wise choice of materials (417).

417

416   In the room of a small Danish girl built-in cabinets take the place of bulky furniture. The width of the room just permitted the bed to be placed below the window. The bed, which serves as a couch in the daytime, leaves ample floor space for playing. Unfortunately the drop-front desk had to be built-in some distance away from the window, but a fluorescent lamp supplements the insufficient daylight over the desk.

417   The warm color of the wood gives this small room the character of a cozy hermitage. Only the light color of the beechwood used for the cantilevered table top contrasts with the pine boarding of the room. There is a small compartment, also of light wood, which opens out at the head of the bed and provides some shelf space.

418

418 The American boy who lives in this room must be grateful to his understanding parents for placing his bed in this adventurous position. A thick foam-rubber mattress and a desk have been placed on a platform. A climbing rope and horizontal bar enable the child to get up and down in sporting style. The space below the two platforms is ideal for storing toys. The colored doors of the built-in fittings give the room depth.

419

419-428   The examples on these pages illustrate rooms for teenagers; neither lavish in size nor in furnishing. Some of them were furnished with the plainest of furniture that is quite obviously secondhand. But imagination and improvisation give these rooms a personal atmosphere, one of freshness and spontaneity. As the illustrations show, young people are receptive to the atmosphere and effects of contrast which can be introduced into modern rooms by antiques such as mirrors or clocks.

419   A Swedish room for a teenage girl, furnished with much love, little money, and an adventurous use of color. The windows are framed top and bottom by projecting boards. On the wall to the right of the window are adjustable shelves clipped into perforated metal rails. The wall on the left of the window is painted navy blue. An old table has been made into a desk by the addition of a top piece; next to it is a reading corner with a cane easy chair, a radio, and a record player on the elongated window sill. Above the bureau, which has been enlivened by turquoise drawer fronts, hangs an old oval mirror. The ensemble makes a gay scheme in spite of its widely disparate elements.

420 Although the different components of this room look rather improvised, the color scheme has been carefully harmonized, and there is a warm, cozy atmosphere. The light tones of the woodwork and the different shades of white stand out well against the background of the dark gray carpet. A simple dressing table has been made of a board attached to the bureau, a rectangular mirror, and a brass candleholder; the whole enlivened by a few trifles. The old-fashioned barometer is an original way of decorating a wall.

421 A spacious room, in which a dressing table and desk have been fashioned of planks laid on top of three cupboard units. The color scheme is predominantly red, blue, and white: apart from the bright blue wall, the other walls and the floor have been kept pale, with a few strong color accents.

420

421

In modern children's rooms built-in table tops nearly always take the place of free-standing tables. This device keeps the center of the room free of bulky furniture and provides a larger working surface, as it usually runs from wall to wall and allows built-in drawer units to go underneath. In this way the child really has a complete work place with everything he needs for homework, hobbies, or painting near at hand. The best place to fix the desk top is near the window with the light falling from the left. Artificial light should come from the same direction. Glare-free hanging lamps or lamps with hinged arms are most suitable. If the working surface must unavoidably be placed against a side wall rather than near a window, one can at least install book shelves with lamps attached above the desk.

It is important to leave enough leg room when determining the height of the table top and particularly when installing cabinets. It is equally important to insure firm support for the table top, as it is virtually inevitable that it will sometimes be used as a seat. The table surface should be able to stand up to rough treatment. There are various ways of protecting it against scratches and stains, from painting with colorless enamel to covering it with laminated plastic.

422

423

422   A simple twin desk. The top is fixed to the wall and the double-decker bed and is also supported by steel sections. Pine has been used for the table and bed; the bed-covers are red and black. The walls are covered with washable plastic pegboard. The curtains, as in most similar schemes, hang down as far as the sill only, to permit objects to be kept on the sill or desk. Hanging lamps have been fixed to a horizontal bar above the curtain rail.

423   Twin desks with drawer units beneath; one of which projects beyond the table top. The desk top is covered with yellow linoleum. Two small compartments reach to the level of the sill, beneath which horizontal strip lights have been fitted. This type of lighting, however, often has a reflection tiring to the eyes.

424 A desk as part of a wall unit. The table top rests on the same wooden brackets as the wall shelves, but it is both wider and deeper. From the point of view of lighting, it is badly placed in the dark corner of the window wall, with daylight coming from the right. The angle lamp at the left, however, is fixed in the correct position for artificial lighting.

424

425

425 A working surface for two on a side wall at the same height as the window sill, supported by tubular steel brackets. On the right the top is cut to allow the door to open. From the point of view of lighting this is a practical scheme, as the daylight comes from the left. Good artificial lighting is provided by hanging lamps. The wall area is used for shelves.

426

427

426, 427   Two rooms on the ground floor of a house built on a hillside have been furnished for teenagers. The rooms have the same floor plan and furniture but are arranged quite differently. Each contains a divan bed, a desk, and a comfortable deskchair on casters. Each has a closet by the door, with a mirror either on the outside or within. Wall-to-wall gray carpets cover the floors. Although the top example leaves less free space, it is preferable, as the desk is lighted from above. In addition, the disadvantages of having a bed immediately below the window and next to the radiator were avoided.

428

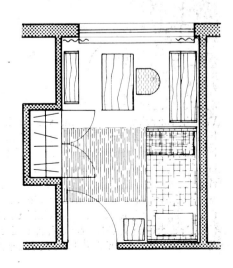

428 Wherever possible, young people should be given everything that makes their room a place of their own. This bed-sitting room for a sixteen-year-old contains features which recall a one-room apartment (463, 464). The desk and handicraft corner is below the window. The bookshelves on the ladder frame run up to room height. The lower cabinet unit with sliding doors accommodates painting materials. A set of low shelves to the left of the desk contains various other items in boxes of different colors. The bed, which can be transformed into a comfortable sofa during the day by the addition of a bolster, stands at the front of the room. If friends come, the room is large enough for them to sit around on stools and cushions. A closet that continues up to the ceiling has been built into the left-hand wall. The lively color scheme is most successful.

429

430

429-432   Some suggestions on where to keep toys and books. Whichever scheme is appealing, from the simple wall shelf to the tall, built-in cabinet, one compartment within easy reach should always be left for the child himself to look after. Experienced mothers and child psychologists agree that children should learn to be tidy from the start. Toy chests and drawers alone are not suitable for this, as most of their contents fall about in a heap when moved. A shelf, on the other hand, encourages a child to move things about, to group them according to size or color, and to reserve special places for favorite toys. Out of the pleasure of arranging grows a sense of order.

431

432

429   A book tree whose shelves are supported by wooden wedges at the back. The vertical board which is the 'trunk' is fixed to the wall at the top.

430   The lowest shelf in the living room has been made available for this little boy. Here he can look after his toys, and it is easy for his parents to enforce the rule that he must not touch the other shelves, even if they are not as far out of reach as in this case.

431   The largest part of this built-in cupboard is used as a dolls' house, with a room on each shelf. This part of the cupboard is closed off by a sliding door with a blackboard surface.

432   The proportions and gay coloring of this furniture make it suitable for a nursery. To the left in the recess are two open compartments serving as a wardrobe and shelves.

Study and hobby room

433 A small studio was made in the large living room of a New York apartment by inserting a partition wall. The furniture was chosen with the purpose of providing enough working surface and space for a designer's books and painting materials. An individual note has been introduced into this rather sober study by a number of original touches.

Study and hobby room

Parlor, study, boudoir, and music room – all these were firm conceptions in our grandparents' time which constituted essential elements in the planning of a middle-class home. Today, in the age of the small apartment, the combined living-dining room, two bedrooms, kitchen, and bath are the norm to which most people must adhere. Even the much joked about and criticized front parlor has given way to the multi-purpose living room, which has to fulfill a number of functions that were formerly divided among several rooms. It is without doubt a great gain that the stiff and sumptuous pomp of bygone days has given way to a much more informal and casual way of living, which is reflected in the flexible way we furnish our homes today. Yet, no matter how versatile we make these multi-purpose rooms, we so often wish for one more to serve needs other than the elementary ones of living, eating, and sleeping. We want a room to which one can retire, either to chat with friends away from the family bustle, or to work quietly, pursue a hobby, or simply to relax. - a room which in a way has the function of the old-fashioned drawing room, study, boudoir, or music room, but which may be furnished entirely according to personal wishes independent of fashion or social requirements. It could take the form of a study, with a desk, bookcase, and perhaps a divan to serve as a bed for a guest. A piano for which there is no room in the living room could here become a center for playing music in the home – a custom that is unfortunately dying out. A collector might choose to furnish this room as a little museum to display his favorite pieces and contain his reference books. Finally, such a room could be used for hobbies. Fathers and sons could work undisturbed at carpentry without interfering with the activities of the rest of the family. A housewife who likes to sew could place a sewing machine and a large table for cutting patterns in this extra room. The great advantage of a workroom is that work can be interrupted and left half-finished without having to be cleared away immediately.

Where there is an extra room available these possibilities should be considered, for often it is only due to lack of imagination that the formal study or somewhat unnecessary dressing room has been revived. If it is fairly clear as a matter of course that a modern apartment with more than three rooms should have one of the smaller ones turned into a hobby room, this principle is even more apparent in a house or spacious old apartment. A small study can be partitioned off from a large room or at the end of a passage. It is even easier to make a new room in a house where an attic or a basement can be adapted to his purpose. The illustrations on the following pages are not intended to serve as rigid models, since the rooms and individual tastes differ in every case. They are merely meant to indicate how solutions have been found in different situations and should certainly provide a host of ideas.

434

434   The study is a room one can decorate entirely according to whim without attention to fashion or the tastes of others. The enormous desk made from a baking trough, the large wine bottle that serves as a lamp, the old garden chair, and the watering can with its ears of grain – all these naïve but eloquent items create a pleasant and relaxing atmosphere for their owner.

A room constructed in the attic provides ideal conditions for anyone who appreciates the charm of sloping ceiling and exposed beams. The difficulties of placing furniture in attic rooms are usually easily overcome, for studies do not require a complicated furnishing scheme. Whether the room is furnished with the simplest pieces from a junk shop or with built-in chests and shelves designed to counterbalance the rooms' irregularities, the structural frame will in either case impart an atmosphere of intimacy and protection.

435 This attic study, the workroom of a shoe designer, looks gay and decidedly rustic. The beams were stained dark, and the walls and ceiling were white washed to make the room appear larger. The old-fashioned bureau was painted white as well. A narrow antique table runs the whole length of the window. Further storage space was made by installing continuous shelves above and below the windows. At the back of the room (not visible here) is a little workshop.

435

436

436 This study in the attic of a private house was planned when the house was built and was provided with a large window on one gable wall (just discernible on the illustration by the shadow thrown on the cabinet). These ideal lighting conditions permitted the whole room, apart from the vertical walls, to be lined with wood. Narrow boards have been used on the ceiling and floor, and walnut veneer has been applied to the built-in cabinet. Adjustable shelves on slotted uprights permit a most successful arrangement on the rear wall: files, books, photographs, and architectural models have been combined to form a lively composition.

A study which not only serves for private correspondence but also accommodates files, books, and a typewriter must be as functional and well planned as a kitchen. Here, as in a kitchen, the flexibility of the units invites variation in design.

437

438

437, 438   The usually narrow dimensions of rooms which have been partitioned off pose particularly vexing problems. The desks in these two examples had to be placed against the long wall and therefore do not get much daylight. Glare-free lamps provide good illumination on the writing surface, and in any case these studies are usually used only in the evening. A certain advantage in these tiny rooms is that everything is within reach. In the upper example one has only to turn around on the revolving chair to reach the desk from the typing table. All the furniture is made of enameled steel, while the table tops are covered with plastic. In the lower example (438) a desk, drawer unit, wall cabinet, and two comfortable chairs have been accommodated in the minimum of space. The walls above the tables are lined with pegboard, which not only serves as a bulletin board for decorations and notices but also improves the acoustics of small rooms.

439   A Swedish architect made his study in an alcove of his large living room. Drawings and plans are kept in fittings that run continuously along the three walls. The bookshelf, also continuous, frames the window opening and repeats the shape of the alcove. An easy chair and a fur rug complete the scheme, which matches the room it adjoins in the choice of materials.

440   The shelves have been carefully planned in this Italian designer's study. The two swivel lamps have been set in grooves in the metal uprights so that they can spotlight any part of the room. The large desk top set beneath the bookshelves provides enough space for a typewriter, telephone, and papers.

441–443 This studio was furnished for a Paris designer with a small living area toward the back of the room. The inadequacies of the old building are hardly noticeable thanks to clever furnishing. The desk (441) is near the balcony door to take full advantage of the daylight. Drafting table and chest of drawers are the same width as the wall projection; the cover of the tall radiator has been cut to follow the angle of the wall. All equipment is housed in a large built-in cabinet covered by a curtain, whose edge forms a kind of chimney corner (442) in the living room. Work and leisure areas are divided by a shelf unit set at angles to the room.

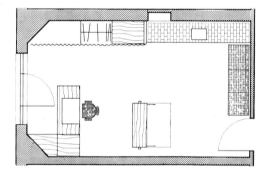

441

442

443

444

444   That an office can be a designer's best advertisement is demonstrated by this studio of an interior decorator. Every visitor is struck by the effective color composition of the rear wall. The striking arrangement recalls modern exhibition techniques. On closer inspection one realizes that the arrangement of furniture has been planned to harmonize with a bold geometric scheme. It was important to create storage space for plans, tracings, tools, and samples. The deep lower cabinets in teak with drawers of different heights provide ample space, supplemented by the wall cabinets with colored plastic sliding doors. The side walls have been incorporated into the well-arranged scheme. Instruments may be hung and designs may be pinned up for scrutiny on the pegboard above the drafting table, while the cork board at the right is used for memos and notices. The room derives much of its character from the color scheme and clever lighting. Two strip lights provide diffuse but bright illumination near the cabinets. The lower one runs beneath the wall cabinets behind an opaque glass pane and illuminates the working surface. The other is hidden by a screen and illuminates the drawers, cabinets, and the ceiling.

A study should be a room for relaxation as well as a place for undisturbed work. If one has enough space one can create out of an extra room an intimate retreat that caters solely to the needs and interests of its occupant. The illustrations on these two pages show a room constructed in the roof space for the owner of an Italian house. This is where he withdraws when he wishes to pursue his scientific interests, to read, to listen to records, and to chat with his friends.

445

446

447

445–447 This example, also illustrates, as do many of the Italian examples featured here, the striking self-assurance of an arrangement in which antique and modern furniture, old and contemporary works of art exist side by side and increase each other's effectiveness. The size of the room is not as big as it may seem, as the window wall is less than seventeen feet long. The arrangement of the furniture makes the room look spacious, and this effect is heightened by a rising ceiling. All tall pieces of furniture – the bookshelf, the loudspeaker installation next to it, and the narrow Spanish table in front were placed against the end wall (447). The Gothic marble sculpture is a focal point for the room. The rest of the room is furnished with low pieces: upholstered chairs on steel frames that can be moved and rearranged at will, and a comfortable rocking chair (445). A radio-phonograph (446) juts out at right angles to the window wall to indicate a division of work and leisure areas. A narrow marble shelf below the window provides space for records and collector's pieces. Lighting is confined to the essential desk lamp and one Japanese paper lantern hung from the ceiling, diffusing a soft light.

448

The two studios on this page are characterized by a clear, matter-of-fact atmosphere. They were furnished in such a way as to be suitable both professionally as architects' offices and privately for study and discussions in a small circle.

448   The large picture-window looking toward the garden gives this room a Japanese character and at the same time insures excellent lighting. The drafting table was moved well back in the room so that the sitting area could be placed by the window. The settee in a slight recess, a table which can be extended by pulling out two leaves, and two simple wooden armchairs provide a comfortable spot for conferences. The settee can also be used as a spare bed. The bookcase has been built along the whole width of the low side wall to save space; its deep shelves are designed to accommodate professional journals and art books.

449

449   A room of marked simplicity. The bookcase of narrow shelves on a slender steel frame stands out as a light silhouette against the dark wall. At table height it was widened to provide a capacious counter. The desk has been pushed right up to the window. At night the fluorescent tubes are augmented by lights set in the sloping ceiling.

450

451

450   In this small room the thick folds of the heavy curtain, the compact book wall, and the comfortable settee combine to produce a study with both personality and warmth. Details such as wicker filing baskets and the old office swivel chair round out this impression. The lighting of the desk has been well solved by glare-free strips beneath the sloping magazine rack.

451   A bed settee, a sewing table, a desk, and a piano had to be accommodated in a Swedish housewife's study. These requirements have been fulfilled through the carefully planned exploitation of space by simple means. The settee was put into an alcove which also houses bookshelves. In front of it stands the sewing table with a basket for mending. The extended window sill makes a well lighted writing surface.

In an art collector's home, the walls of every room reveal his passionate pursuit, but for relaxation or concentration he prefers to withdraw to his study. Here he keeps his extensive reference library and contemplates the favorite pieces of his collection.

452   The same sense of pure order that pervades the other rooms of his apartment (200–202) can be found in the study of a New York architect and art collector. Throughout the apartment white painted walls provide a neutral background for the frequently changing display of pictures. The large bookshelf built into the alcove is divided up quietly and unobtrusively by the uniform arrangement of the shelves. Large volumes lie flat in low compartments. The chest of drawers on the left accommodates a collection of prints. Its depth is determined by the size of the items in this collection and provides ample space for an uncrowded display of sculptures. A low chest has been placed against the end wall, which leaves most of the wall free for hanging large paintings. The white marble tops of the desk and shelf match those in the living-dining room. The standard lamp with its pivoting reflectors can illuminate both the desk and the armchair and table.

452

453

453   The special charm of this study derives from its situation in the small
gallery of a two-story living room. The high, sloping ceiling creates an effect
of spaciousness despite the room's narrow width. A bookcase running the
whole length of the side wall was set directly on the floor. The desk, placed
at right angles to the fireplace wall and hence out of sight of the living room,
punctuates the long axis. The armchair near the banister has a view of both
the gallery and the room below. The standard lamp can be turned to illuminate different parts of the room as required. The improvised arrangement
of the pictures contributes much to the lively character of the study and
affords a better viewing angle for the spectator who wishes to examine them.

Even in a small house an area for writing and sewing should if possible be provided for the housewife. There she will be able to leave any work when interrupted without having to clear it away as she would in another part of the house. These two examples from Scandinavia prove how pleasant solutions can be found at low cost and with simple furniture.

454

454 Very different pieces were chosen for the furniture in the study corner of this Stockholm flat. A simple wooden typing desk stands in front of the blue wall beneath a series of homemade shelves. The little sitting area by the window is charming and lively, with its various elements such as the rocking chair, a low table with filigree frame, and a second chair of wood and leather. The angle lamp and the low hanging lantern are suitable lighting fixtures for this corner. The country-style willow basket next to the wooden chair is a nice touch and is used as a container for newspapers.

455

455 This sewing corner is simple but practical. The white plastic table top has a scratch-resistant surface. When the table is required for sewing or cutting material, the little extension leaf provides additional space. The narrow bureau with gaily painted drawers and the bright lampshade give the whole corner a fresh appearance.

456

456   This example shows how an extra room in a large apartment has been
made into a study. The clever arrangement of comfortable settee, reading
corner, and work area with desk and bookcase gives the room a neat appearance. The desk and shelves have been assembled from standard parts.
Their slender steel framework and the alternation of black and white shelves
bring an air of lightness and elegance into the room. The radio and magazines are within reach of the couch. The built-in cabinets along the window
wall not only provide room for filing photographic prints and negatives but
afford additional space for standing things along the continuous top.

457

458

The workshop means more nowadays than just an appendage to the rest of the house. Certainly, it saves time and money when the master of the house can carry out small repairs and when the housewife can make clothes for herself and the children. But this by no means entails any real need of a separate, well organized place for such activities. For most people the advantage of having manual skills lies in the relaxation they bring rather than their practicality or convenience. Coupled with this is the creative joy of having fashioned something with one's own hands – however imperfectly – a satisfaction that even children value very highly. In families that take pleasure in manual activities, no trouble should be spared to create the right background for them. It is comparatively easy to add a workshop to private houses where the attic (457) or the basement (460) affords enough space. But quite often the workshop is planned as part of a new house, either as a separate room (458) or as an alcove opening directly onto the living room (459).

457   This versatile and spacious workshop was constructed in an attic with the simplest means. The two large, well-lit tables provide plenty of space for writing, sewing, and repair work. The wooden surfaces rest on metal supports at the right and on a shelf at the left and may be lifted off easily to leave the room empty for games.

458   This workshop in the small house of a Swedish couple is equally well planned. The wood paneling creates a quiet atmosphere, brightened by plastic tops and gaily colored curtains.

459

460

459   This workshop, which is almost the size of a small carpentry shop, has been incorporated into the living room. Though it is marked off by a woven slat screen and a plain softwood floor, it still offers a surprise view into the world of work. This contrast gives the house a peculiar charm while illustrating at the same time the essential role played by leisure activities in the home.

460   This workshop has been installed in a basement, for the two sons of the owner; while not very large, it is quite adequate and well equipped. The long narrow room was fitted at one end with closets, where clothes can be put away in moth balls and where ironing can also be done.

461

461 This bed-sitting room in an American nurses' home is entered via a small ante-room which contains closets. The room has been very clearly arranged. There is a small desk against the wall on the left that is separate from the sitting area consisting of a divan, shelf unit, small mosaic table, easy chair, and stool. The dining alcove, in the immediate proximity of the kitchen, has been distinguished from the rest of the room by its floor tiles and blue walls.

The small apartment

The small apartment

The one-room apartment is a problem posed by the changed social structure of our times. Single people who lead an independent existence and no longer live with their families, people who live in the country but want a *pied-à-terre* in town, young couples whose financial position does not allow them a larger place, all manage to make comfortable homes within the restrictions of a one-room apartment. The reason they can do this successfully is that nowadays apartments are designed with flexibility to suit individual tastes.

The one-room apartment gives independence to all those who would otherwise have to live in furnished rooms. It combines all the functions of living in a confined space and therefore the utmost care is required in planning it. Living, working, sleeping, and dining are the functions of the main room. Only rarely is a separate bed-recess provided. For cooking there is nearly always a separate alcove. The incorporation of a dining area in the kitchen is only possible in larger apartments. Adequate built-in cabinets are essential to avoid having a wardrobe in the living room and to overcome the perpetual problem of insufficient storage space.

ingenious exploitation of the space available is as much the occupant's concern as the architect's. Where a door opens immediately into the bed-sitting room without a hall or anteroom, an attempt should be made to hide part of the room from the view of the person who enters (478). Even in smaller rooms, different functions can divide the room up into zones (464, 465) and a subdivided scheme looks bigger. Tall furniture such as bookcases, which in a large room can be set at right angles to the wall as a room divider, should be placed against the wall in a small apartment. In small rooms couches, low shelf units, or tables can form or accentuate groups. Sometimes carpets or rugs suffice to define an area. Multi-purpose furniture such as convertible sofas, beds which store in wall cabinets, expanding tables, and retractable shelves are practical and solve most of the problems of limited space. The furnishing of hotel rooms, where similar problems are encountered, had already pointed the way even before the one-room apartment became an accepted building type.

Visual lightness, which is the trend in modern furniture, is particularly suited to the demands of the one-room apartment. Overstuffed chairs and massive chests fill the room more than filigree tubular steel chairs, suspended shelves or low cabinets on narrow bases, even if they take up the same amount of floor space. It is difficult, moreover, to incorporate antique furniture in tiny apartments as it nearly always needs a sizable room to set off in proper scale. It is important to think of the effect that color will have when deciding on a scheme. Red and warm orange, which make the room look smaller, can be used only where proportions must be corrected (465) or where the room is big enough to make such considerations unnecessary. In any case, bright colors must be used with care, and large areas in neutral shades should balance them, not only for spatial but also for psychological reasons. A color scheme suitable for a living room is not necessarily appropriate for a bedroom. The same applies to the patterns on upholstery, curtains, wallpapers, and carpets. The subdivisions which are usual to denote the manifold functions of one-room apartments must not be emphasized by a restless décor.

462

462 The one-room house represents an extreme. This example of a glass house stresses the simple beauty of open space and shows the ultimate development of combining all the activities of living in one large room. Only the bathroom is separate in a kind of inner cell. The precision of the sections used, the encircling glass walls, the extreme simplicity of the furniture, and the use of the most costly materials create an ascetic luxury which can only be realized in exceptional cases and must be justified by the owner's sumptuous style of living. An extensive site that will insure privacy is a further prerequisite.

463

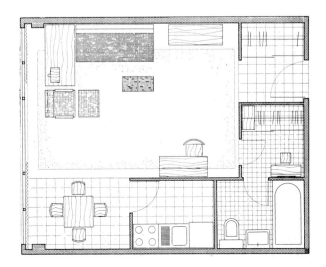

463 Living area of the apartment shown in
example 461. The divan has been made into
a bed. The dining table is of walnut on
a white metal frame. The table by the
window features a travertine slab and a
walnut shelf on a black enameled steel frame.
Carpet and upholstery are in fine-grained
black and white; the curtain running across
the whole window wall is in four colors,
predominantly blue and green. The adjoining
areas of the apartment are grouped around
the main room. The kitchen opens off the
dining area; the dressing room with its
dressing table gives access to the bath and is
entered from the living area.

464

465

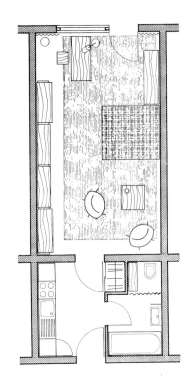

464, 465   The furniture of this apartment on the top floor of a skyscraper had to fit into long narrow rooms with a very limited living area. The divan subdivides the room into living and working areas, each with its own light fixtures; one zone features two shell-shaped chairs and a plastic-topped table, and the other has a low filing cabinet and a desk with the light coming from the left. The bed and work table are of ash, while the filing cabinet, chair, and storage wall are of teak. Apart from the colors of the wood three other colors are dominant: the vermilion red of the curtain, which brings the far wall nearer, the blue-green of the divan, and in the darkest part of the room, the bright yellow of the chair. The gray fiber rug provides a good neutral tone to set off the color scheme.

466

467

468

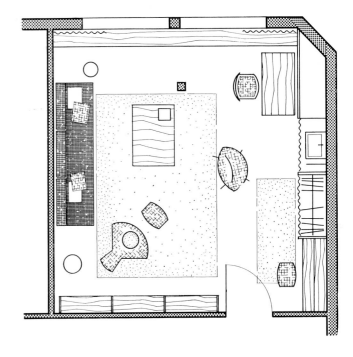

469

466-469 Two tiny attic rooms in a Paris apartment house were combined to make up one almost square room. The rectangular column is the only trace of the demolished partition wall. The cozy character of the small room is emphasized by shaggy natural wool rugs. Here again gray is the background color: dark wall-to-wall carpets, a mouse-gray wall, and a couch and chair covered with a black and white checked material. Color accents are provided by a blue curtain, an orange chair and stool, and various bright cushions. The wooden parts of the table, desk, and wall shelf are made of cherrywood. Essential storage space, sink and kitchenette are hidden behind a woven slat curtain.

470

470-472 This Swedish apartment is distinguished by an informal atmo-sphere of considerable flexibility. The tea table and a small box unit run on casters and may be combined with the couch or the divan (which also serves as a bed) to make up a sitting area. The metal frames of the long table against the wall, a chair with an adjustable back, and the swivel lamp have a slightly technical appearance, but their filigree construction is graceful and elegant. The color scheme ranges from off-white and yellow to a warm mid-brown and gray, with greens in the chair cover and lamp shade.

471 A small adjoining room permitted the kitchen to be supplemented by a dining recess near the window, with a circular table and four black chairs. The main room accordingly does not need to be used for dining so that no large table was required there.

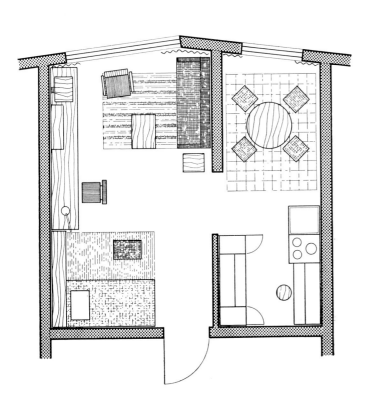

471

472

473

473, 474 The same apartment as in Figs. 470–472 looks completely different with other furniture. The central features are now firmly fixed: four bentwood chairs around a circular dining table, a blue divan, a blue and red stool, and a smoky plastic table top on white angle supports. Both areas are defined by woven straw floor mats. A straw mat attached to the wall behind the divan provides a vertical accent. The predominant color is golden yellow, especially when the sunlight filters through the yellow curtains. Suspended lamps hung at different levels provide a rhythmic note. As in the previous example, no cabinets were needed since there is enough storage space in an anteroom.

474

475

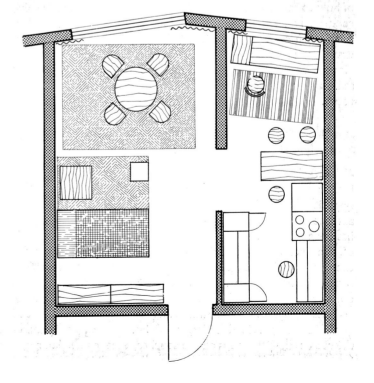

475 The extra room, with the kitchen in the front as in Fig. 471 has a working area by the window. A unit with drawers on the left and a table top set a little below it provide a lighted place for the owner to do household jobs and sew. The remaining space was utilized for a breakfastbar, which saves serving the smaller meals in the dining area.

476

476-479   One-room apartments for married couples require consideration
of the different interests of the owners. In a larger apartment, the problem
of how to make separate working and living areas is easily solved. In a one-
room apartment this requirement must be met by a subdivision of space. In
the French example (476, 477) it has been achieved by installing a sliding
door between the living room and the study situated in an anteroom. The
German apartment from the Berlin Interbau Exhibition (478, 479) has the
same aim of separating the different living areas in one large, continuous
room.

477

476, 477   The great advantage of this apartment inhabited by a young couple
is the extensive storage space provided by built-in cabinets along the wall
opposite the window in the bed-sitting room, and on the long wall of the
anteroom. A studio couch, which can be made into a double bed at night,
has been set into the cabinet wall of the main room. A sliding door sections
off the anteroom, which includes a bathroom and kitchen (not visible in
the photograph) and a small desk with its own light. In the foreground is a
sitting area with two small tables which can be pushed together and a
dining area with four shell-shaped chairs. By keeping the sliding door open
and making use of the couch in front of the cabinet wall in the anteroom,
seating can be provided for larger parties. Some charming materials enliven
the room: sheepskin rugs on the couches, a shaggy woolen rug on top of the
fitted carpet, and timber veneer on walls and cabinets.

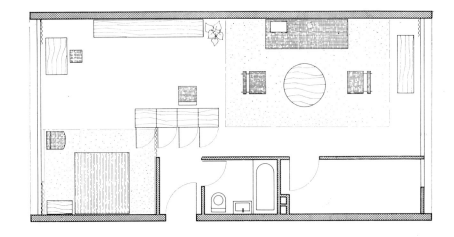

478

479

478, 479 The layout of this plan – apart from bath and kitchen – was left to the tenants and their interior decorator. The latter has used cabinets to form a room-dividing wall. This, together with a short wall near the front door, creates a little hall which takes the place of a vestibule. The spaciousness of the room is preserved by the use of low furniture; areas are formed by the grouping of the furniture. The dining area is near the kitchen. A sitting area, with a divan, round mosaic table, easy chairs on tubular steel legs, and a radio-phonograph, is placed to take advantage of the light streaming through the window. Shelf units and a desk below the north window constitute the owner's study. A second broad divan that serves as a bed at night has been placed in the alcove to the left of the front door. The timbers used are teak and ash; the divan is covered with black wool, and the chairs are lilac and burgundy.

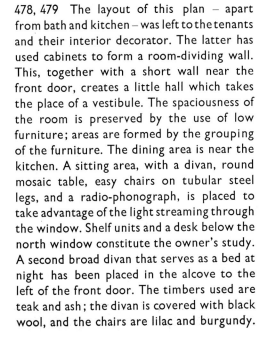

480

481

480–483 A bed-sitting room, whose furniture has been designed so that it can easily be used in different rooms at a later stage. Even the suspended rosewood cabinets can be used independently. The installed wooden partition behind the bookshelves has been fixed to a metal frame, as the existing wall could not carry the weight of the books. The low cabinets beneath the window accommodate the bedding during the day. There is room for a coat closet behind the enlarged Piranesi engraving, which is fixed on

483

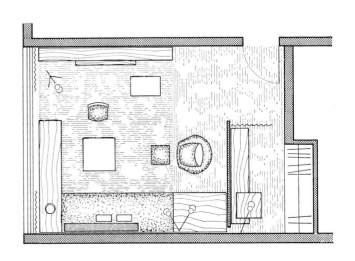

gle irons. In addition to the standard lamp and adjustable
ll lights, concealed fluorescent bulbs extend the whole
gth of the room and illuminate the bookwall in particu-
. A navy-blue fiber carpet runs across the black floor
er, while turquoise-blue fabric is used on the wall
hind the divan. Armchair and stool are bright red, and
e divan is covered in dull yellow. All these colors are
eated in the checks of the curtain. The window is fitted
h white Venetian blinds. The table-tops are travertine.

484

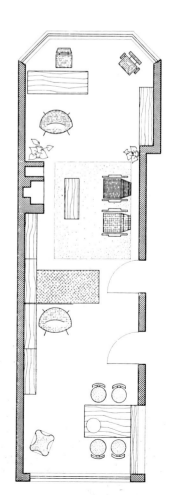

484–488   This apartment was created in a narrow Dutch house by making a few structural changes. The long narrow room, which, following Dutch tradition, runs the whole depth of the house, is divided up into two almost equal parts by a sliding rush mat. One section of the room is for living, working, and sleeping and the other for dining. The arrangement of the furniture in the living area is determined by the large fireplace. The open fire, the built-in log compartment next to it, and the rough-hewn stones are intended to convey a feeling of shelter and protection. The rectangular arrangement of the seats is softened by the casual distribution of the lamps. A bay window accommodates the desk made of a heavy board on a white-enameled steel frame, a chair, and a built-in cabinet with a magazine rack at the right. A couch forms the division from the other area, but the storage wall continues on beyond the rush mat. The marble top of the dining table projects through the serving hatch into the adjoining kitchen. A cabinet unit accessible from both kitchen and dining room has been built into the wall between them.

485

486

487

488

489

490

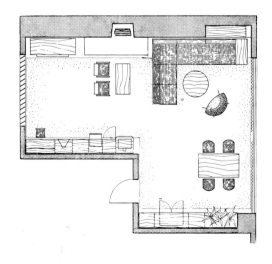

489–494 This spacious one-room apartment for a young actress in New York would satisfy the most fastidious requirements. It has sufficiently large adjoining areas – dressing area, bath, and kitchen – to obviate the need for cabinets in the main room and so establish the generous effect of empty space. Both the dining area, placed near the kitchen with a well-equipped bar, and the sitting area, consisting of two couches at right angles, a table, and a chair, command a fine view over Central Park through the wide windows. The back rest of the settee projecting into the room is adjustable (489, 490). Thus it serves as a seat not only for conversations in the living corner but also for chats around the fire. At the same time, the couch can also be related to the two 'music centers' of the room, the piano by the fireplace wall and the combined radio-television set and phonograph opposite. The custom-made music cabinet beneath the shelf combines a number of different units: a television set on a turn table that can swivel to the correct viewing angle, a record player, a radio, and a small desk.

491

492

493

494

INDEX OF ARCHITECTS AND DESIGNERS

ACKNOWLEDGMENTS

The authors' thanks are due to the following institutions, architects and photographers for permission to reproduce their work:

Amann, Norbert, Munich 31, 32, 34-36
Andresen, Th., Farum, Denmark 168
(from his book Blumenfenster, published by Georg D. W. Callwey, Munich), 175, 394, 460
Apel, Otto, Frankfort-on-Main 81
Artecasa, Milan 440
Arts Ménagers, Paris 138, 139, 305, 323-326, 342, 401, 423, 441-443

Bennett, Ward, New York 69
Beyda, Janet & Frank, Paris 6, 27, 67, 68, 94-99, 238-242, 328, 329, 336-339, 348-353, 445-447
Bildarchiv Foto Marburg 16
Binder, Heinz A., Stuttgart 388
Binder, Walter, Zurich 30, 150
Braun, Max, Frankfort-on-Main 126
Breuer, Marcel, New York 57
Brugger, Albrecht, Stuttgart 230

Carver, Norman F., Kalamazoo, USA 17
Casali, Giorgio, Milan 3
Clari, Davide, Milan 412-415
Conard, Erich, Stockholm 50, 51, 151, 159, 180-182, 191, 205, 206, 209, 210, 215, 287, 290, 294, 295, 301, 302, 327, 341, 376, 377, 392, 404, 405, 419, 421, 435

Conzett & Huber, Zurich 193-196
(Photo: J. Bräm)

Damora, Robert, Bedford Village, USA 105
Dassas, N., Paris 148
Daube, Christian, Berlin 149
Dearborn-Massar, New York 82, 176 284, 286, 309-315
Deyhle, Ernst, Rottenburg a. N. 47, 87, 88, 197, 250-254, 258, 259, 316, 453
Domus, Milan 85, 86, 135-137, 143, 144, 190, 431

Ellegaard Foto, Copenhagen 223-225, 370, 416, 448

Fachklasse für Fotografie, Kunstgewerbeschule Zurich 320
Femina, Hälsingborg 289, 293, 469-474
Finsler, Hans, Zurich 300
Fotogramma, Milan 44, 45, 48, 123, 157, 158, 203, 204, 303
Frattini, Gianfranco, Milan 29

Gaynor, Frank L., Tucson, Okla. 282
Georges, Alexandre, Hewlett, USA 131, 132, 488-493
Göllner, Max, Frankfort-on-Main 76, 174, 449
Gorne, J., Paris 466-469
Guhl, Emil, St Gallen 385, 386

Hafner, Leo, Zug 111
Hansen, Erik, Copenhagen 63, 266, 267, 292, 379, 380, 422, 424, 425
Harvey, Robert D., Boston 188, 189
Havas, Heikki, Helsinki 64, 219, 220, 271, 306, 307, 390, 395, 408
Hecht, Munich 65
Hedrich-Blessing, Chicago 463
Heidersberger, H., Brunswick 41, 436
Heinemann, Hans-Erlich, Skövde, Sweden 91, 285, 439
Helmer-Petersen, Keld, Copenhagen 5, 26, 115, 247-249, 278
Hervé, Lucien, Paris 18
Hoffmann Verlag, Stuttgart 28 (from Gute Möbel – Schöne Räume), 394 and 407 (from Wohnen in Skandinavien)
Høm, Jesper, Copenhagen 4
Hyde, Scott, New York 24, 58, 79, 361, 381

Jacobsen, Palle, Roskilde, Denmark 226
Johansson, Sven-Gösta, Stockholm 66, 154
Jonals Co., Copenhagen 1 (from Danske Møbler, publ. Gjellerups Forlag)

Kayaert, R., Brussels 255-257
Kessler, Rudolf, Berlin–Wilmersdorf 321, 477, 478
Knoll Associates, New York 8, 10, 60, 61, 243-246, 319
Knoll International, Stuttgart 59, 146
Knöppel, Ulf, Stockholm 123, 167, 179, 264, 273, 275, 276, 396, 420, 430, 455, 456
Köster, Walter, Berlin 172, 216, 322, 358, 391, 459

Lazi, Franz, Stuttgart 54, 89, 90, 438
Leloir, Jean-Pierre, Paris 333

SUBJECT INDEX